Flask

Web Framework

Building Interactive Web Applications with SQLite Database

A Practical, Hands-on Guide for Beginners to Intermediate

Developers, Including Real-World Projects and Step-by-Step

Instructions for Creating Dynamic and Engaging Web Experiences

Mark John P. Lado, MIT

ISBN: 9798309496099

Imprint: Independently published

DEDICATION

To the aspiring data scientists, developers, and machine learning engineers who seek to translate complex models into real-world solutions: This book is dedicated to you. It is born from the belief that data science shouldn't exist solely in notebooks, but rather be accessible and impactful through interactive web applications. May this guide illuminate the path, demystifying the integration of machine learning with Flask, and empowering you to build applications that not only predict but also inform, engage, and ultimately, make a difference. From laying the foundations with Flask fundamentals to mastering advanced techniques like API design, asynchronous tasks, and robust security practices, this book aims to equip you with the practical skills and knowledge necessary to bring your data-driven visions to life. May your journey from model to web app be filled with discovery, innovation, and the satisfaction of creating something truly useful.

ACKNOWLEDGMENT

This book wouldn't have been possible without the support and inspiration of many individuals. I extend my sincere gratitude to the vibrant Python and Flask communities, whose open-source contributions and collaborative spirit have been invaluable. I am deeply thankful to the authors and maintainers of the numerous libraries and frameworks that form the backbone of this work, including Scikit-learn, Pandas, NumPy, Plotly, Bokeh, and countless others. Their dedication to creating powerful and accessible tools has made this journey significantly smoother. I also acknowledge the contributions of online tutorials, documentation, and forum discussions that have shaped my understanding and approach to web development and machine learning integration. Finally, I want to thank my family and friends for their unwavering support and encouragement throughout this project. Their belief in me has been a constant source of motivation.

TABLE OF CONTENTS

This page is intentionally left blank

Part I

Foundations

CHAPTER 1

INTRODUCTION TO WEB

DEVELOPMENT

HOW THE WEB WORKS

Let's delve into the fascinating world of web development by exploring how the web actually functions. Imagine you're sitting at your computer and you decide to visit a website, say, www.example.com. This seemingly simple action initiates a complex chain of events. First, your browser needs to translate the human-readable domain name, www.example.com, into a numerical IP address, which is like the postal code for a server on the internet. This is where the Domain Name System (DNS) comes into play. Your computer contacts a DNS server, which acts like a phone book for the internet, and asks it for the IP address associated with www.example.com. This process might involve multiple DNS servers communicating with each other to find the authoritative answer. Once your computer has the IP address, it can establish a connection with the server hosting the website. This connection typically uses the Hypertext Transfer Protocol (HTTP), which defines how messages are formatted and transmitted over the internet (Fielding et al., 1999). You can think of HTTP as the language that your browser and the server use to communicate. Your browser sends an HTTP request to the server, essentially asking for the web page. This request might be a GET request, if you're simply viewing the page, or a POST request, if you're submitting a form. The server then processes the request and sends back an HTTP response, which contains the web page's HTML, CSS, and JavaScript files. Your browser then interprets these files and renders the web page for you to see. This entire process, from typing the URL to seeing the website, relies heavily on these interconnected systems working seamlessly. A question that often arises is, "What happens if the DNS server is down?" In such a scenario, your computer wouldn't be able to resolve the domain name to an IP address, and you'd likely see an error message. A practical solution is to use a different DNS server, perhaps one provided by a public DNS service like Google Public DNS (8.8.8.8 and 8.8.4.4) or Cloudflare DNS (1.1.1.1 and 1.0.0.1). Understanding these fundamental concepts is crucial for any aspiring web developer, as they form the bedrock upon which all web applications are built. Further exploration of HTTP methods, status codes, and the intricacies of TCP/IP will build a more robust understanding of web communication.

Introduction to Backend Development

Backend development plays a critical role in creating dynamic and data-driven web applications. While frontend development focuses on the user interface and user experience, backend development handles the server-side logic, data storage, and business rules that power the application. Imagine an e-commerce website. The frontend allows users to browse products, add them to their cart, and proceed to checkout. However, the backend is responsible for managing product information, processing orders, handling user accounts, and ensuring secure transactions. Without a robust backend, the frontend would be merely a static display, unable to perform any meaningful actions. Backend development addresses several key problems. First, it provides a centralized and secure location for storing and managing data. Databases, such as relational databases like PostgreSQL (Stonebraker & Neuhold, 2010) or NoSQL databases like MongoDB (Chodorow, 2010), are used to organize and persist data. Second, backend systems handle the business logic of the application. For example, in the e-commerce scenario, the backend would calculate discounts, manage inventory, and generate invoices. Third, backend development provides APIs (Application Programming Interfaces) that allow the frontend to communicate with the server. These APIs define how data is exchanged between the frontend and the backend. We need servers to host these backend applications and make them accessible to users over the internet. Servers are essentially computers with powerful hardware and specialized software that are designed to handle multiple requests simultaneously. Real-world examples of backend systems are abundant. Consider social media platforms like Twitter or Facebook. Their backend systems manage user profiles, handle posts and comments, maintain connections between users, and deliver personalized content. Streaming services like Netflix or Spotify rely on backend systems to manage their vast libraries of content, handle user subscriptions, and deliver media streams to users. Online banking platforms require highly secure backend systems to manage financial transactions and protect sensitive user data. A common question is, "Why not just store all the data in the browser?" The answer lies in security, scalability, and data integrity. Storing sensitive data in the browser is highly insecure, as it can be easily accessed and manipulated. Furthermore, browsers have limited storage capacity, making it impractical to store large amounts of data. Finally, maintaining data consistency across multiple users would be extremely difficult without a centralized backend system. Therefore, backend development is essential for building modern, scalable, and secure web applications.

WHY FLASK?

Flask, often described as a "microframework" for Python web development, offers a different approach compared to more comprehensive frameworks like Django. This distinction stems from their differing philosophies regarding included functionality and default project structure. Flask intentionally keeps its core lean, providing only the essential tools for routing requests and working with templates. This minimalism offers several advantages. Firstly, it gives developers greater control over the components they choose to integrate. If your project requires a specific database library or authentication system, Flask allows you to select and implement it without being tied to Django's defaults. This flexibility is particularly valuable for smaller projects or those with very specific requirements. Secondly, Flask's smaller codebase often translates to faster learning and quicker development cycles, especially for developers already familiar with Python. You're not burdened by learning a large, opinionated framework's conventions if your application remains relatively simple. Thirdly, the microframework nature of Flask makes it ideal for building APIs or microservices, where a full-fledged framework might be overkill. Imagine building a simple backend API to serve data to a mobile app; Flask's lightweight nature makes it a perfect fit.

However, Flask's minimalism also presents some disadvantages. The "batteries not included" approach means developers must often assemble the necessary components themselves, which can increase development time for larger, more complex projects. Django, on the other hand, comes with a wealth of built-in features, including an ORM (Object-Relational Mapper) for database interactions, a powerful templating engine, and an administrative interface. These features can significantly accelerate development for complex web applications, reducing the need to reinvent the wheel. For example, if you are building a large e-commerce platform with user authentication, product management, and payment gateway integration, Django's built-in features and established project structure would likely be more beneficial (Lattner, 2015). A common question is, "When should I choose Flask over Django, and vice-versa?" A good rule of thumb is to consider the scale and complexity of your project. For smaller projects, APIs, or applications with specific component requirements, Flask's flexibility and simplicity make it a strong choice. For larger, more complex projects where rapid development and a comprehensive set of tools are crucial, Django's "batteries included" approach is often more advantageous. It's also worth noting that Flask's flexibility allows it to scale effectively even for complex applications, as demonstrated by platforms like Pinterest, which initially leveraged Flask (High Scalability, 2011). The key is to choose the framework that best aligns with the project's current and anticipated future needs.

SETTING UP YOUR DEVELOPMENT ENVIRONMENT

Setting up a robust development environment is a critical first step for any web developer. A key practice in this process is the use of virtual environments. Imagine you're working on multiple projects, each requiring different versions of libraries. Installing these libraries globally could lead to conflicts, where one project's dependencies break another. This is where virtual environments come to the rescue. A virtual environment is an isolated Python environment that allows you to install packages specific to a project without affecting other projects or your system's Python installation. Tools like venv (Python's built-in solution) or virtualenv create these isolated spaces (Python Packaging Authority, n.d.). This ensures that your project dependencies are managed cleanly and consistently, preventing the dreaded "dependency hell." A common question is, "Why not just use Docker?" While Docker containers offer another level of isolation, virtual environments are generally preferred for local development due to their lighter weight and faster setup. Docker is more commonly used for deployment and production environments.

Beyond virtual environments, the choice of development tools significantly impacts productivity. While a simple text editor can suffice for basic tasks, Integrated Development Environments (IDEs) like VS Code or PyCharm offer a wealth of features that streamline the development process. These IDEs provide code completion (IntelliSense), debugging tools, version control integration (Git), and project management capabilities. For instance, VS Code's IntelliSense can predict what you're typing, reducing typos and speeding up coding. PyCharm's debugger allows you to step through your code line by line, making it easier to identify and fix bugs. These features not only save time but also improve code quality. While some developers prefer the simplicity of text editors like Sublime Text or Atom, IDEs are generally recommended, especially for beginners, as they provide a more supportive and feature-rich development experience. My preferred setup often involves VS Code for its versatility and extensive plugin ecosystem, combined with a virtual environment for each project. I also recommend familiarizing yourself with Git from the start, as version control is essential for collaborating on projects and managing code changes effectively (Chacon & Straub, 2014). Learning to use a linter like Pylint or Flake8 can also help catch potential code issues early on. Ultimately, the best development setup is the one that works best for you, but embracing virtual environments and leveraging the power of IDEs are highly recommended practices for any web developer.

CHAPTER 2

YOUR FIRST FLASK

APPLICATION

CREATING A BASIC FLASK APP

Let's dive into creating our very first Flask application. A fundamental concept in Python, and crucial for Flask, is the __name__ variable. When you execute a Python script directly, the __name__ variable is set to __main__. However, when you import that script as a module into another script, the __name__ variable is set to the name of the module. This distinction is particularly important in Flask because Flask needs to know where your application's code resides. When you create a Flask app instance, you typically do so like this: app = Flask(__name__). By passing __name__ to the Flask constructor, you're telling Flask where to find templates, static files, and other resources related to your application. This becomes especially critical when you start organizing your Flask application into multiple files and packages. Without the correct __name__, Flask might not be able to locate these resources correctly, leading to errors.

Consider a scenario where you have a Flask application with templates stored in a templates folder. If you were to run your Flask app directly, __name__ would be __main__, and Flask would correctly locate the templates folder relative to the main script. However, if you were to import this Flask app into another script and try to run it from there, __name__ would be the name of the imported module, not __main__. Without passing the correct __name__ when creating the Flask app instance, Flask might look for the templates folder relative to the importing script, which could lead to a TemplateNotFound error. A common question is, "What happens if I don't include __name__?" While some basic Flask apps might appear to work without it, especially in simple single-file applications, it's a best practice to always include it. Relying on implicit behavior can lead to unexpected issues as your application grows and becomes more complex. Furthermore, some Flask extensions might rely on __name__ to function correctly. Therefore, explicitly passing __name__ ensures that your Flask application behaves consistently, regardless of how it's run or imported. This principle extends beyond just templates; it's crucial for managing static files (CSS, JavaScript), configuration files, and other resources associated with your Flask app. By consistently using app = Flask(__name__), you establish a clear and reliable foundation for your Flask projects.

Understanding Routes and Decorators

In Flask, routes are the mechanism by which we define which URLs should trigger which functions in our application. This connection between URLs and functions is elegantly achieved using decorators, a powerful feature in Python. Decorators are essentially a way to modify or enhance functions in a clean and reusable manner. They wrap a function with another function, adding functionality before or after the original function is executed. The @app.route decorator in Flask is a prime example of this. Let's break down how it works. When you use @app.route('/hello') above a function like def hello_world():, you're telling Flask that whenever a user visits the /hello URL, the hello_world function should be executed. The @app.route decorator registers this association between the URL and the function within Flask's routing system. It's important to understand that decorators are executed when the function is *defined*, not when it's *called*. This means that the routing rules are set up when your Flask application starts. A common question arises: "How does Flask know which function to call when a user visits a URL?" Flask uses the information provided by the @app.route decorator to build a routing table. When a request comes in, Flask looks up the requested URL in this table and executes the associated function.

Beyond the commonly used GET method, which is used for retrieving data, HTTP offers several other methods, each with a specific purpose. POST is used for submitting data to the server, such as form submissions. PUT is used for updating existing data, while DELETE is used for removing data. Flask allows you to specify which HTTP methods a route should handle using the methods argument in the @app.route decorator. For example, @app.route('/submit', methods=['POST']) would only handle POST requests to the /submit URL. If a user tries to access this URL using a GET request, they would receive a "Method Not Allowed" error. Using appropriate HTTP methods is crucial for building RESTful APIs (Richardson & Ruby, 2002), which are a common pattern for web applications. RESTful principles emphasize using HTTP methods in a standardized way to represent actions on resources. For instance, a POST request to /users might create a new user, while a GET request to /users/123 might retrieve information about the user with ID 123. Understanding how decorators work and how to use different HTTP methods is fundamental for building robust and well-structured web applications with Flask.

RETURNING RESPONSES

While returning simple strings from a Flask view function is common for basic examples, Flask is capable of handling a much wider range of data types. Beyond strings, you can return responses as dictionaries, lists, tuples, or even custom objects. Flask automatically converts these data types into appropriate HTTP responses. For instance, returning a dictionary will often be automatically formatted as a JSON response, which is particularly useful when building APIs. You can also return more complex data structures, and Flask, with the help of extensions or manual serialization, can convert them into formats like XML or other custom formats. This flexibility in handling data types makes Flask suitable for building a variety of applications, from traditional web pages to sophisticated data-driven APIs.

Furthermore, controlling HTTP status codes is essential for providing meaningful feedback to the client and for proper error handling. While Flask implicitly sets a 200 OK status code for successful responses, you often need to return different status codes to indicate various situations. For example, a 404 Not Found status code should be returned if the requested resource is not found, a 400 Bad Request if the client made an invalid request, or a 500 Internal Server Error if something went wrong on the server. Flask allows you to set HTTP status codes explicitly by returning a tuple from your view function. The tuple should contain the response body and the desired status code. For example, return jsonify({'message': 'Resource not found'}), 404 would return a JSON response with a 404 status code. Using appropriate status codes is crucial for building robust and well-behaved web applications. They provide valuable information to clients about the outcome of their requests and allow clients to handle different situations gracefully. A common question is, "Why not just always return a 200 OK status code?" While it might seem simpler, doing so would obscure the actual status of the request. For example, if a user tries to access a non-existent page and you return a 200 OK, the client might assume the request was successful, leading to confusion. Proper use of status codes is a key aspect of building RESTful APIs (Fielding, 2000) and ensuring interoperability between different systems. They allow clients to understand the semantics of the response without needing to parse the response body, making your applications more predictable and easier to integrate with.

RUNNING THE DEVELOPMENT SERVER

When developing a Flask application, you'll often use the built-in development server. This server, while convenient for local testing, is not designed for production use. A key feature often used during development is the debug=True setting. Enabling debug mode has several important consequences. First, it automatically reloads the server whenever you make changes to your code. This means you don't have to manually restart the server every time you modify a file, significantly speeding up the development process. Imagine you're tweaking the styling of your website; with debug=True, you can simply save the CSS file, refresh your browser, and see the changes instantly. Second, debug mode provides a more informative debugger in your browser if an error occurs. Instead of a generic error message, you'll often see a detailed traceback, pinpointing the exact line of code causing the problem. This makes it much easier to diagnose and fix bugs. A common question from beginners is, "Why doesn't debug mode show me *all* the variables and their values?" While debuggers can be powerful, they generally don't expose every single variable at every point in the execution for performance and security reasons.

However, the information they provide is usually sufficient to identify the root cause of most errors.

However, the very features that make debug=True so helpful during development make it extremely dangerous in a production environment. The automatic code reloading can introduce security vulnerabilities, as it might reload code that has been modified maliciously. Moreover, the detailed error messages displayed in the browser in debug mode can expose sensitive information about your application's internals, such as file paths, database queries, or configuration settings. This information could be exploited by attackers. Therefore, it is absolutely crucial to *never* run a Flask application with debug=True in production. In a production setting, you should use a production-ready WSGI server like Gunicorn or uWSGI, which are designed for performance, stability, and security (The Pallets Projects, n.d.). These servers handle requests more efficiently and provide better control over the application's lifecycle. They also allow you to configure logging and error handling in a way that's suitable for a production environment. A good practice is to have separate configuration files for development and production, where debug=True is set only in the development configuration. This ensures that you don't accidentally deploy your application with debug mode enabled. Understanding the difference between the development server and production-ready servers, and the implications of debug=True, is essential for deploying secure and reliable Flask applications.

CHAPTER 3

WORKING WITH

TEMPLATES

INTRODUCTION TO HTML TEMPLATES

Templates are a fundamental concept in web development, especially when using frameworks like Flask. They offer a clean and efficient way to generate HTML dynamically, separating the presentation of your web pages from the underlying application logic. Imagine building a website that displays a list of products. You could technically construct the HTML directly within your Flask code using string concatenation or f-strings. However, this approach quickly becomes cumbersome and difficult to maintain, especially as the complexity of your HTML grows. Templates provide a much better solution. They are essentially HTML files with placeholders for dynamic content. Flask then uses a templating engine, like Jinja2, to populate these placeholders with data from your application. This separation of concerns, where HTML structure resides in templates and Python code handles the logic, offers several significant benefits.

First, it improves code organization and readability. By separating HTML from Python, you make your code easier to understand and maintain. Frontend developers can work on the templates without needing to understand the intricacies of the backend code, and vice-versa. This facilitates collaboration between different team members. Second, templates promote code reusability. You can create reusable template components, like headers, footers, or navigation bars, and include them in multiple pages. This reduces code duplication and makes it easier to update the look and feel of your website consistently. Third, templates enhance security. Templating engines often provide built-in mechanisms for escaping potentially dangerous characters in user-provided data, preventing cross-site scripting (XSS) vulnerabilities (OWASP, 2023). Directly embedding user data into HTML can make your application vulnerable to XSS attacks, where malicious scripts injected by users can be executed in other users' browsers. A common question is, "Why not just use a JavaScript framework for rendering the UI?" While JavaScript frameworks are powerful for building complex interactive UIs, templates still play a crucial role, especially for server-side rendering. Server-side rendering with templates can improve initial page load times and SEO, as search engines can more easily crawl and index the content. Furthermore, templates can be combined with JavaScript frameworks to create powerful hybrid applications. For example, you might use templates for the initial rendering of the page and then use a JavaScript framework to handle dynamic updates and interactions. Therefore, understanding and utilizing templates is an essential skill for any web developer working with Flask or similar frameworks.

THE TEMPLATES DIRECTORY

Flask's convention of looking for templates within a directory named "templates" stems from its design philosophy of providing sensible defaults while still allowing for customization. This convention simplifies project structure and makes it easier for developers to organize their template files. When you render a template using render_template('index.html') in your Flask view, Flask, by default, searches for index.html within the "templates" directory located in the same directory as your main Flask application file. This predictable location helps maintain consistency across Flask projects and makes it easier for developers to understand the project layout. Imagine you're working on a team project; everyone knows that the HTML templates reside in the "templates" folder, making it easy to find and modify them.

However, Flask's flexibility allows you to deviate from this convention if needed. You can configure the template folder by modifying the template_folder argument when creating your Flask application instance. For example, app = Flask(__name__, template_folder='html_templates') would tell Flask to look for templates in a directory named "html_templates" instead of "templates." This can be useful if you want to organize your templates differently or if you're integrating Flask with an existing project that has a different directory structure. A common question is, "Why would I want to change the default template directory?" One scenario is when you have a large number of static files, including HTML, CSS, JavaScript, and images. You might want to organize these files into different subdirectories, and you might prefer to keep your HTML templates in a subdirectory within a "static" folder, for instance. Another scenario is when you are working with a frontend framework that already has a defined directory structure for templates. Changing the template_folder allows Flask to seamlessly integrate with such frameworks. It's important to note that changing the template folder requires you to be consistent throughout your application. Whenever you use render_template, you should be aware of the configured template_folder to ensure Flask correctly locates your templates. While the default "templates" directory is generally recommended for its simplicity and consistency, Flask's ability to customize the template folder provides the flexibility needed to adapt to different project requirements and organizational preferences.

Rendering Templates with

RENDER_TEMPLATE()

The render_template() function in Flask is the bridge between your Python code and your HTML templates. It's the mechanism by which you dynamically generate HTML pages by combining template files with data from your application. Behind the scenes, render_template() leverages Jinja2, a powerful and flexible templating engine, to achieve this. When you call render_template('index.html', name='John'), Flask first locates the index.html file within the configured template directory (usually the "templates" folder). Jinja2 then parses this template file, looking for any placeholders or template expressions enclosed in double curly braces {{ ... }} or {% ... %}. These placeholders represent where the dynamic data from your Python code will be inserted.

In our example, {{ name }} in index.html would be a placeholder. render_template() takes the keyword arguments you provide (in this case, name='John') and makes them available to the template. Jinja2 then replaces the {{ name }} placeholder with the value 'John'. This process creates a fully rendered HTML string, which is then returned to the client's browser as the response. A crucial aspect of render_template() is that it handles the complexities of interacting with the Jinja2 templating engine. You don't need to manually deal with loading templates, parsing them, or substituting values. render_template() abstracts all of that away, providing a clean and simple interface. A common question is, "What happens if the template file doesn't exist?" In such a scenario, Flask will raise a TemplateNotFound exception, which you can handle gracefully in your application using error handling mechanisms. Another question is, "How can I pass more complex data structures, like lists or dictionaries, to the template?" render_template() can handle these as well. You can pass lists and dictionaries as keyword arguments, and then access their elements and properties within the template using Jinja2's templating syntax. For example, if you pass a list of users, you can iterate over it in your template using Jinja2's for loop construct. Understanding how render_template() works and how it interacts with Jinja2 is fundamental for building dynamic and data-driven web applications with Flask. It provides a clean and efficient way to separate presentation from logic, making your code more maintainable and easier to work with.

PASSING DATA TO TEMPLATES

Dynamically displaying data in templates is at the heart of creating interactive and personalized web experiences. Jinja2, the templating engine used by Flask, provides a powerful and intuitive syntax for achieving this. We pass data from our Flask view functions to the templates using keyword arguments in the render_template() function. These keyword arguments become accessible as variables within the template itself. For example, if we call render_template('profile.html', username='Alice', age=30), the profile.html template can then access these values using double curly braces: {{ username }} would display "Alice", and {{ age }} would display 30. This mechanism allows us to easily inject data into our HTML, creating dynamic content like user profiles, product listings, or news feeds. Imagine building an e-commerce site; you could pass a list of products from your Flask view to the template, and then use Jinja2's looping constructs to display each product's name, price, and image.

Now, let's clarify the difference between {{ variable }} and {% block %} in Jinja2. {{ variable }} is used for *outputting* the value of a variable. It's a way to embed Python expressions directly into the HTML. Jinja2 evaluates the expression and inserts the result into the rendered

HTML. This is how we display dynamic data, as described above. {% block %}, on the other hand, is used for *template inheritance*. It's a powerful feature that allows you to create reusable template structures. You define a base template with certain blocks, which are essentially placeholders for content. Then, you can create child templates that inherit from the base template and override or extend these blocks. This is incredibly useful for maintaining consistency across your website. For instance, you might have a base template with a header, footer, and navigation bar. Then, each page on your site can inherit from this base template and just define the content specific to that page within a block. A common question is, "Can I use Python code directly inside the template?" While Jinja2 allows for some limited expressions, it's generally best practice to keep complex logic in your Python view functions and only use the template for presentation. This separation of concerns makes your code cleaner, more maintainable, and easier to test. Another question is, "How do I handle errors or missing data in my templates?" Jinja2 provides filters and conditional statements that allow you to handle these situations gracefully. For example, you can use an if statement to check if a variable exists before displaying it, preventing errors if the data is missing. Mastering how to pass data to templates and understanding the difference between {{ }} and {% %} are essential skills for building dynamic and maintainable web applications with Flask.

TEMPLATE INHERITANCE

Template inheritance is a powerful feature in Jinja2, and by extension, Flask, that significantly enhances code reusability and maintainability in web development. Imagine you're building a website with multiple pages, each sharing a common layout, including a header, footer, navigation bar, and perhaps a sidebar. Without template inheritance, you'd have to duplicate this HTML structure on every single page, leading to a lot of redundant code. This makes updating the layout a nightmare; if you want to change the navigation bar, you'd have to modify it in dozens of different files. Template inheritance solves this problem elegantly. It allows you to define a base template containing the common layout elements, and then create child templates that inherit from this base template. Child templates can then override or extend specific sections of the base template, customizing the content while preserving the overall structure.

Think of it like a master blueprint for your website's layout. The base template acts as this blueprint, defining the overall structure. Individual pages then use this blueprint as a starting point, customizing only the parts that are unique to them. This dramatically reduces code duplication. Instead of repeating the header and footer HTML on every page, you define them once in the base template and simply include them in the child templates. This makes your code much cleaner and easier to manage. Furthermore, template inheritance significantly improves maintainability. If you need to update the header or footer, you only need to make the change in one place – the base template – and the changes will automatically propagate to all the child templates that inherit from it. This eliminates the risk of inconsistencies and ensures that your website has a unified look and feel. A common question is, "How does Jinja2 know which parts of the base template to override?" Jinja2 uses {% block %} tags to define these overridable sections. In the base template, you define blocks with names, and in the child templates, you can redefine these blocks with new content. Jinja2 then intelligently merges the base template with the child template, replacing the original block content with the new content from the child template. This mechanism allows for granular control over which parts of the layout are customized. Template inheritance is a cornerstone of building scalable and maintainable web applications. It promotes DRY (Don't Repeat Yourself) principles, reduces code duplication, and simplifies the process of updating and maintaining website layouts. By leveraging template inheritance, developers can focus on the unique content of each page without having to repeat the common structural elements, leading to more efficient and less error-prone development.

JINJA2 TEMPLATING ENGINE BASICS

Jinja2's power lies not just in inserting variables into HTML, but also in its robust set of control structures that allow for dynamic HTML generation. These structures, including loops and conditionals, enable us to create templates that adapt to different data and conditions, making our web pages interactive and data-driven. Imagine building a product catalog; you wouldn't want to manually write the HTML for each product. Jinja2's for loop comes to the rescue. You can pass a list of products from your Flask view to the template, and then use the {% for product in products %} construct to iterate over each product. Inside the loop, you can access the product's properties (name, price, image) and display them within HTML elements. This dynamic generation of HTML based on data is a fundamental concept in web development, and Jinja2 makes it remarkably easy.

Beyond loops, conditional statements ({% if condition %}) are equally crucial. They allow you to display different content based on certain conditions. For example, you might want to display a "Login" button only if the user is not logged in, or show a special offer banner only during a promotional period. Jinja2's if statements allow you to implement this logic directly within your templates. You can use comparison operators, logical operators, and even check for the existence of variables to create complex conditions. A common question is, "Can I nest loops and conditionals?" Yes, Jinja2 supports nested loops and conditionals, allowing you to create even more complex dynamic HTML structures. For instance, you could have a nested loop to display products within different categories. Another question is, "How can I handle situations where data might be missing?" Jinja2 provides filters that can be used to handle such cases. For example, the default filter allows you to specify a default value if a variable is not defined. This prevents errors and ensures that your templates handle all possible data scenarios gracefully. Mastering Jinja2's control structures is essential for building dynamic and interactive web applications. They allow you to create templates that adapt to different data and conditions, making your web pages more engaging and user-friendly. By combining loops, conditionals, and filters, you can create templates that are both powerful and maintainable, significantly simplifying the process of building data-driven web applications.

EXERCISE

Let's solidify our understanding of template inheritance and data passing by outlining a practical exercise: creating a multi-page website with a consistent layout. Imagine building a simple blog. We'll want a header with the blog title, a navigation bar, a main content area, and a footer with copyright information. Template inheritance is the perfect tool for this. First, we'll create a base template, perhaps named base.html. This template will contain the HTML structure for the header, footer, and navigation bar. We'll define blocks within this base template, such as content, where the content of individual pages will go. The header and footer will be consistent across all pages, so they'll be defined directly in the base.html template.

Next, we'll create individual templates for our blog posts, perhaps index.html for the main page and post1.html, post2.html, etc., for individual posts. These templates will *inherit* from base.html using the {% extends "base.html" %} directive at the top of each file. Within these child templates, we'll redefine the content block with the specific content for that page. This allows us to keep the common layout elements from base.html while customizing the content area for each post. Now, the crucial part: passing data from our Flask routes to these templates. Let's say we want to display the blog title in the header and the post title and content in the individual post templates. In our Flask view functions, we'll use render_template() to render the appropriate template, passing the data as keyword arguments. For example, in a route that handles displaying a specific post, we might call render_template('post1.html', blog_title='My Blog', post_title='First Post', post_content='This is the content of my first post.'). These variables – blog_title, post_title, and post_content – will then be accessible within the template using double curly braces, {{ ... }}.

A common challenge beginners face is ensuring the correct paths for template inheritance. Remember that Flask looks for templates in the "templates" directory by default. So, base.html, index.html, and post1.html should all reside within this directory. Another potential issue is forgetting the {% extends %} directive in the child templates. Without it, the child templates won't inherit from the base template, and the layout won't be applied correctly. This exercise helps solidify the concepts of template inheritance and data passing, demonstrating how to create a consistent layout across multiple pages while dynamically populating the content with data from Flask routes. It's a fundamental pattern for building any multi-page web application and

provides a solid foundation for more complex templating techniques.

CHAPTER 4

HANDLING USER INPUT

WITH FORMS

CREATING HTML FORMS

HTML forms are the primary way users interact with web applications, providing a mechanism to submit data to the server. They are composed of various input fields, each designed for a specific type of data. Understanding the different input field types and how to use them effectively is crucial for building interactive and user-friendly web applications. Common input types include text for single-line text input, password for secure password entry, email for email addresses, number for numerical input, checkbox for selecting multiple options, radio for selecting a single option from a group, select for dropdown menus, and textarea for multi-line text input. Each input type has specific attributes that control its behavior and validation. For example, the required attribute makes an input field mandatory, while the min and max attributes define the allowed range for numerical inputs. Imagine building a registration form; you would likely use text inputs for name and address, an email input for email, a password input for password, and perhaps checkbox inputs for accepting terms and conditions.

Two essential attributes for any HTML form are method and action. The method attribute specifies how the form data should be sent to the server. The two most common methods are GET and POST. GET appends the form data to the URL as query parameters, which is suitable for small amounts of data and is generally used for retrieving data. POST, on the other hand, sends the form data in the body of the HTTP request, which is more secure and can handle larger amounts of data. POST is typically used for submitting data, such as form submissions or file uploads. The action attribute specifies the URL where the form data should be sent. This is the URL of the server-side script or endpoint that will process the form data. For instance, in a login form, the action attribute might point to a URL like /login, which is handled by your Flask application. A common question is, "When should I use GET vs. POST?" A general guideline is to use GET for retrieving data and POST for submitting data. GET requests are also generally idempotent, meaning that making the same GET request multiple times should have the same effect. POST requests, on the other hand, are not necessarily idempotent. Another question is, "How can I validate form data on the client-side?" HTML5 provides built-in validation attributes like required, min, max, and pattern that can be used to perform basic validation in the browser. JavaScript can also be used for more complex client-side validation. However, it's crucial to remember that client-side validation is not a substitute for server-side validation, as it can be bypassed by malicious users. Therefore, always validate form data on the server to ensure data integrity and security. Understanding the different input types, the method and action attributes, and the importance of both client-side and server-side validation are fundamental for building secure and user-friendly web forms.

HANDLING FORM SUBMISSIONS

When dealing with form submissions in web applications, understanding the distinction between GET and POST requests is crucial. These two HTTP methods serve different purposes and have distinct characteristics that influence their suitability for various scenarios. GET requests are primarily used for retrieving data from a server. When a user submits a form using the GET method, the form data is encoded into the URL as query parameters, appended after the base URL. For example, if a user searches for "shoes" on an e-commerce site, the URL might look like /search?q=shoes. This makes GET requests easily bookmarkable and shareable, as the search query is directly embedded in the URL. However, because the data is in the URL, there are limitations on the amount of data that can be sent, and sensitive data like passwords should *never* be transmitted via GET. Furthermore, GET requests are generally considered idempotent, meaning that making the same GET request multiple times should have the same result.

POST requests, on the other hand, are designed for submitting data to a server. When a form is submitted using POST, the data is included in the body of the HTTP request, rather than the URL. This makes POST requests more suitable for larger amounts of data, such as form submissions, file uploads, and complex data structures. Critically, because the data is not exposed in the URL, POST is the appropriate method for transmitting sensitive information. Imagine a user logging into a website; their username and password should be sent via POST to prevent them from being visible in the URL or browser history. POST requests are not necessarily idempotent; submitting the same POST request multiple times might have different effects, such as creating multiple identical entries in a database. A common question is, "Why not just use GET for everything?" The key difference lies in security and data capacity. Exposing sensitive data in URLs is a major security risk. Furthermore, the URL has a limited length, making GET unsuitable for large data submissions. Another question is, "How does Flask access the form data sent via POST?" Flask provides the request.form object, which is a dictionary-like object containing the submitted form data. You can access individual form fields using their names as keys, for example, request.form['username']. In summary, GET is appropriate for retrieving data and is often used for search queries or accessing specific resources, while POST is the correct method for submitting data, especially sensitive information or large amounts of data, and is the standard for form submissions. Choosing the correct method is crucial for building secure and functional web applications.

ACCESSING FORM DATA

Accessing form data in Flask is fundamental to processing user input and building dynamic web applications. Flask provides the request object, which contains all the information about the incoming request, including the form data. The primary way to access form data submitted via POST is through request.form. This object behaves like a dictionary, where the keys are the names of the input fields in your HTML form, and the values are the corresponding user-submitted data. For example, if your form has an input field named "username," you can access the submitted username in your Flask view using request.form['username']. It's important to note that request.form will only contain data submitted via POST. If the form is submitted using GET, the data will be in the URL as query parameters, and request.form will be empty.

For data submitted via GET, Flask provides request.args. This object also behaves like a dictionary and contains the query parameters from the URL. So, if a user visits /search?q=shoes, you can access the search query "shoes" in your Flask view using request.args['q']. The key difference between request.form and request.args is the HTTP method used to submit the data. request.form is for POST data (typically form submissions), while request.args is for GET data (typically query parameters in the URL). A common question is, "What happens if a user submits a form field with the same name multiple times (e.g., multiple checkboxes with the same name)?" In this case, request.form will return a list of values for that field name. You can then iterate over this list to access each individual value. Another crucial point is security. Always sanitize and validate user input before using it in your application. Never trust user-provided data, as it could contain malicious code or invalid characters. Failing to sanitize input can lead to vulnerabilities like cross-site scripting (XSS) or SQL injection attacks. Therefore, always sanitize and validate data accessed through both request.form and request.args to ensure the security and integrity of your application. Understanding the difference between these two objects and implementing proper data sanitization are essential skills for building secure and robust Flask applications.

FORM VALIDATION

Form validation is a crucial aspect of web development, ensuring data integrity and preventing a multitude of potential issues. Without proper validation, your application could be vulnerable to security risks, data corruption, and a poor user experience. Imagine a user submitting a registration form with an invalid email address or a password that doesn't meet the required criteria. Without validation, this bad data could be stored in your database, leading to problems down the line. Form validation acts as a gatekeeper, ensuring that only valid and acceptable data is processed by your application. It also provides immediate feedback to the user, guiding them to correct any errors in their input.

Several common validation techniques exist. These include checking for required fields, validating data types (e.g., ensuring a phone number contains only digits), verifying data formats (e.g., email addresses, dates), checking data ranges (e.g., age must be between 18 and 120), and ensuring data uniqueness (e.g., username must not already exist). These techniques can be implemented both on the client-side (in the user's browser) and on the server-side (on your web server). Client-side validation provides immediate feedback to the user, improving the user experience by catching errors before the form is submitted. This can be achieved using HTML5 attributes like required, type, and pattern, or through JavaScript. However, client-side validation is not foolproof, as it can be bypassed by disabling JavaScript or manipulating the HTML.

Therefore, server-side validation is absolutely essential. This is where you perform the most rigorous validation checks, as you cannot trust data coming from the client. In Flask, you can implement server-side validation within your view functions, checking the data submitted through request.form or request.args. If validation fails, you can return an error message to the user, indicating which fields need correction. A good practice is to provide specific and informative error messages, guiding the user towards submitting valid data. A common question is, "Why do we need both client-side and server-side validation?" The answer is that they serve different purposes. Client-side validation improves the user experience by providing instant feedback, while server-side validation is crucial for security and data integrity. Think of client-side validation as a first line of defense, and server-side validation as the ultimate safeguard. Another question is, "How can I handle validation errors gracefully?" Flask provides several ways to do this, such as using flash messages to display error messages to the user or rendering the form again with the error messages displayed next to the corresponding fields. Implementing robust form validation, both client-side and server-side, is a fundamental aspect of building secure, reliable, and user-friendly web applications.

USING FLASK-WTF

Flask-WTF is a powerful extension for Flask that streamlines the process of working with web forms. It simplifies form creation, rendering, validation, and CSRF (Cross-Site Request Forgery) protection, significantly reducing the boilerplate code you'd otherwise have to write. Imagine building a complex form with multiple fields, custom validation rules, and error handling. Without a form library like Flask-WTF, you'd have to manually create the HTML form, handle form submissions, validate each field individually, and manage error messages. This can quickly become tedious and error-prone. Flask-WTF addresses these challenges by providing a structured and organized way to define and manage forms.

Using Flask-WTF, you define your forms as Python classes, inheriting from FlaskForm. Within this class, you define the form fields as attributes, using classes like StringField, PasswordField, IntegerField, etc., provided by Flask-WTF. You can also specify validation rules directly within the form field definitions using validators like DataRequired, Email, Length, etc. This declarative approach makes your code more readable and maintainable. Flask-WTF then handles the rendering of the HTML form, the processing of form submissions, and the execution of the validation rules. It also provides helpful features like displaying error messages next to the corresponding fields. A key advantage of using a form library like Flask-WTF is that it promotes code reusability. You can define a form class once and reuse it in multiple templates. This reduces code duplication and ensures consistency across your application. Furthermore, Flask-WTF provides built-in CSRF protection, a crucial security measure that prevents malicious websites from forging requests to your application. CSRF attacks are a common vulnerability, and Flask-WTF's built-in protection significantly reduces the risk.

A common question is, "Why not just handle forms manually?" While it's possible to handle forms manually, it requires significantly more code and effort, especially for complex forms. Flask-WTF handles many of the tedious tasks for you, allowing you to focus on the core logic of your application. Another question is, "How does Flask-WTF integrate with my templates?" Flask-WTF provides helper functions that make it easy to render forms in your templates. You can iterate over the form fields and access their attributes, such as labels, values, and error messages. This allows you to create flexible and customized form layouts. In essence, Flask-WTF simplifies form management by providing a structured way to define forms, handle submissions, perform validation, and protect against CSRF attacks. It promotes code reusability, improves maintainability, and enhances security, making it an invaluable tool for any Flask developer working with web forms.

EXERCISE

Let's put our knowledge of forms and validation into practice with a practical exercise: building a user information collection form. Imagine creating a contact form for a website. We want to collect the user's name, email address, and a message. Crucially, we need to validate this data to ensure it's in the correct format and doesn't contain any malicious input. We'll use Flask-WTF to simplify this process. First, we'll define a form class using Flask-WTF. This class will inherit from FlaskForm and will contain fields for name, email, and message. We'll use StringField for the name and message, and EmailField for the email, leveraging Flask-WTF's built-in email validation. We'll also add DataRequired validators to each field to ensure they are not left blank. For the message field, we might add a Length validator to limit the message length.

Next, in our Flask view function, we'll create an instance of this form class. When the user submits the form (via POST), we'll check if the form is valid using form.validate_on_submit(). This function automatically handles the validation process based on the validators we defined in the form class. If the form is valid, we can then process the data, perhaps by storing it in a database or sending an email notification. If the form is invalid, form.validate_on_submit() will return False, and we can access the error messages associated with each field using form.errors. We can then pass these error messages to our template and display them next to the corresponding form fields. In our template, we'll use Jinja2 to render the form fields and display any associated error messages. We can iterate over the form fields and their errors to create a user-friendly display.

A common challenge is ensuring that error messages are displayed correctly next to their respective fields. Flask-WTF makes this easy by associating error messages with the form fields themselves. You can access the errors for a specific field using form.fieldname.errors, where fieldname is the name of the field in your form class. Another point to consider is how to handle different types of validation errors. Flask-WTF provides specific error messages for each type of validation failure, such as "This field is required" or "Invalid email address." You can customize these error messages if needed. This exercise provides a practical example of how to use Flask-WTF to create, validate, and process forms in a Flask application. It demonstrates the power of Flask-WTF in simplifying form management and ensuring data integrity, which are essential for building robust and user-friendly web applications.

PART II

BUILDING INTERACTIVE

WEB APPLICATIONS

CHAPTER 5

WORKING WITH

DATABASES

INTRODUCTION TO DATABASES

Databases are fundamental to modern web applications, providing a structured and persistent way to store, manage, and retrieve data. Without a database, data would be lost every time the application shuts down, making it impossible to build anything beyond the simplest static websites. The benefits of using a database are numerous. First, they provide data persistence, ensuring that data is retained even after the application restarts or the server goes down. Second, they offer efficient data retrieval through indexing and query languages, allowing you to quickly access specific data without having to search through entire files. Third, they provide data integrity through constraints and transactions, ensuring that data is consistent and accurate. Fourth, they enable data sharing and concurrent access, allowing multiple users or applications to access and modify the same data simultaneously. Imagine building an e-commerce platform; you would need a database to store product information, user accounts, orders, and other data, ensuring that this information is persistent, easily accessible, and consistent.

Databases can be broadly categorized into relational databases and NoSQL databases. Relational databases, like PostgreSQL or MySQL, organize data into tables with predefined schemas. They use SQL (Structured Query Language) to interact with the data, allowing for complex queries and joins across multiple tables. Relational databases are well-suited for applications with structured data and complex relationships between data entities, such as financial systems or enterprise resource planning (ERP) systems (Silberschatz et al., 2010). NoSQL databases, on the other hand, offer more flexibility in data structure and do not require a fixed schema. They come in various forms, such as document databases (like MongoDB), key-value stores (like Redis), and graph databases (like Neo4j). NoSQL databases are often preferred for applications with unstructured or semi-structured data, high read/write loads, or when scalability and flexibility are paramount, such as social media platforms or real-time analytics dashboards (Sadalage & Fowler, 2012).

A common question is, "When should I choose a relational database over a NoSQL database, and vice-versa?" The choice depends largely on the nature of your data and the requirements of your application. If you have structured data with complex relationships and require

ACID (Atomicity, Consistency, Isolation, Durability) properties, a relational database is likely the better choice. If you have unstructured or semi-structured data, require high scalability and flexibility, and can tolerate eventual consistency, a NoSQL database might be more appropriate. Another question is, "Can I use both relational and NoSQL databases in the same application?" Yes, it's becoming increasingly common to use a combination of both types of databases, leveraging the strengths of each. For example, you might use a relational database for transactional data and a NoSQL database for analytics data. Understanding the differences between relational and NoSQL databases and choosing the right database for your application is a crucial decision that can significantly impact the performance, scalability, and maintainability of your web application.

SQLite Basics

SQLite, a file-based database engine, offers a unique approach to data storage compared to client-server databases like PostgreSQL or MySQL. Instead of running as a separate process, SQLite embeds directly within the application, storing the entire database within a single file. This embedded nature offers several advantages. First, it simplifies deployment. Since there's no separate server to configure, deploying an application with SQLite is as simple as copying the database file along with the application code. This makes it ideal for small to medium-sized applications, mobile apps, or situations where a full-fledged database server is not feasible or desirable. Second, SQLite is lightweight and requires minimal configuration, making it easy to get started with and suitable for development or prototyping. Third, its file-based nature makes it portable. You can easily move the database file between different systems without needing to export or import data. Imagine building a small personal finance application; SQLite's simplicity and file-based nature make it a perfect fit for storing transaction data locally on the user's computer.

However, SQLite also has limitations. Its file-based architecture makes it less suitable for high-concurrency applications with many simultaneous users. Because the entire database resides in a single file, concurrent write operations can lead to performance bottlenecks. While SQLite can handle a reasonable number of concurrent reads, write operations are serialized, which can become a bottleneck under heavy load. Furthermore, SQLite lacks some advanced features found in client-server databases, such as user management, fine-grained access control, and robust transaction management. A common question is, "When is SQLite a good choice?" SQLite is a good choice for small to medium-sized applications with moderate traffic, mobile apps, desktop applications, prototyping, and situations where simplicity and ease of deployment are prioritized over high concurrency and advanced features. For example, a simple blog, a personal task management application, or a small embedded system might be well-served by SQLite. Another question is, "When should I *not* use SQLite?" If you anticipate high traffic, require advanced database features, or need fine-grained access control, a client-server database like PostgreSQL or MySQL would be a more appropriate choice. In summary, SQLite is a powerful and convenient database engine for specific use cases, but it's essential to understand its limitations and choose the right database for your application's needs.

CONNECTING TO A DATABASE WITH PYTHON

Establishing a connection to a database using Python is the first step towards interacting with and manipulating data. Python provides standard database interfaces through modules like sqlite3 for SQLite, psycopg2 for PostgreSQL, and others for various database systems. The process generally involves importing the appropriate database module, then calling a connection function, passing in the necessary connection parameters. For SQLite, this might look like import sqlite3; conn = sqlite3.connect('mydatabase.db'), while for PostgreSQL it might involve more parameters like username, password, host, and database name. This connection object, often referred to as the database handle, represents the active session with the database. It's the conduit through which all subsequent database operations are performed. Think of it as establishing a phone line to the database server; you need this active connection to communicate.

Once a connection is established, we need a way to execute SQL queries and retrieve results. This is where the concept of a *cursor* comes in. A cursor is an object created from the connection that allows you to traverse and manipulate the data retrieved from the database. You can think of it as a pointer that moves through the result set of a query. You create a cursor object from your connection, for instance, cursor = conn.cursor(), and then use it to execute SQL statements. For example, cursor.execute("SELECT * FROM users") would execute the query and make the results available through the cursor. You can then fetch the results using methods like cursor.fetchone() to retrieve one row at a time, cursor.fetchall() to retrieve all rows, or cursor.fetchmany() to retrieve a specified number of rows.

A common question is, "Why do we need a cursor? Why can't we just execute queries directly through the connection?" The cursor provides an abstraction layer that separates the execution of the query from the handling of the results. This allows you to process the results in a controlled and efficient manner, especially for large result sets. Imagine retrieving thousands of rows from a database; you wouldn't want to load all of them into memory at once. The cursor allows you to fetch and process the results in smaller chunks, preventing memory issues. Another important point is that cursors are often used for parameterized queries, which are crucial for preventing SQL injection vulnerabilities. Instead of directly embedding user input into SQL queries, you can use placeholders and pass the values separately through the cursor, ensuring that the input is treated as data and not as executable code. Understanding how to establish a database connection and use cursors is fundamental for any Python developer working with databases, forming the basis for all database interactions.

EXECUTING QUERIES

Writing SQL queries is a fundamental skill for interacting with databases. The four basic operations—SELECT, INSERT, UPDATE, and DELETE—allow you to retrieve, add, modify, and remove data. Let's consider a scenario involving a simple "users" table with columns for id, username, and email. A SELECT query like SELECT username, email FROM users WHERE id = 1 retrieves the username and email of the user with ID 1. An INSERT query like INSERT INTO users (username, email) VALUES ('newuser', 'newuser@example.com') adds a new user to the table. An UPDATE query such as UPDATE users SET email = 'updated@example.com' WHERE id = 1 modifies the email of the user with ID 1. Finally, a DELETE query like DELETE FROM users WHERE id = 1 removes the user with ID 1 from the table. These are basic examples, and SQL offers much more complex operations, including joins, subqueries, and aggregate functions. Practice writing different types of queries to become comfortable with the syntax and logic.

However, a critical security concern when executing SQL queries is the risk of SQL injection vulnerabilities. These vulnerabilities arise when user-provided input is directly embedded into SQL queries, allowing attackers to manipulate the query and potentially gain unauthorized access to the database. Imagine a web application that allows users to search for products by name. If the search term is directly concatenated into the SQL query, an attacker could enter a malicious search term like ' OR '1'='1, which could modify the query to return all products instead of just the ones matching the intended search term. The most effective way to prevent SQL injection is to use *parameterized queries* or *prepared statements*. Instead of directly embedding user input into the query, you use placeholders, and then pass the values separately to the database driver. For example, in Python with the sqlite3 module, you might do something like cursor.execute("SELECT * FROM products WHERE name = ?", (search_term,)). The ? acts as a placeholder, and the (search_term,) tuple provides the value for the placeholder. The database driver then handles the escaping and quoting of the input, ensuring that it is treated as data and not as SQL code.

A common question is, "Why are parameterized queries so important?" They are essential because they completely separate the SQL code from the user-provided data. This prevents attackers from injecting malicious SQL code into your queries. Another question is, "Are there other ways to prevent SQL injection?" While parameterized queries are the most effective method, input validation and escaping can also provide some level of protection. However, relying solely on input validation or escaping is generally not recommended, as it can be complex and error-prone. Parameterized queries provide a much simpler and more robust solution. Mastering SQL queries and understanding how to prevent SQL injection are fundamental skills for any web developer working with databases. Protecting your database from SQL injection is paramount for the security and integrity of your application.

DISPLAYING DATA IN TEMPLATES

Fetching data from a database and displaying it in HTML templates is a core task in building dynamic web applications. The process generally involves executing a SQL query to retrieve the desired data, then passing that data to the template engine for rendering. Let's imagine a scenario where we have a "products" table in our database, and we want to display a list of products on a webpage. First, in our Flask view function, we would establish a database connection, create a cursor, and execute a SELECT query to retrieve the product data. For example, using SQLite, we might have code like this: conn = sqlite3.connect('mydatabase.db'); cursor = conn.cursor(); cursor.execute("SELECT name, price FROM products"); products = cursor.fetchall(); conn.close(). This code fetches the name and price of all products and stores them in the products variable, which is typically a list of tuples, where each tuple represents a row from the database.

Next, we pass this products data to our HTML template using the render_template() function. For instance, we might call render_template('products.html', products=products). Within the products.html template, we can then use Jinja2's templating engine to iterate over the products list and display the data within HTML elements. A typical Jinja2 loop might look like this: {% for product in products %} <tr> <td>{{ product[0] }}</td> <td>{{ product[1] }}</td> </tr> {% endfor %}. This code iterates over each product in the products list (passed from the Flask view) and displays the product name and price in table cells. The product[0] and product[1] access the elements of the tuple representing each product (name and price, respectively).

A common question is, "How can I display more complex data structures, like dictionaries or objects, in my templates?" You can pass dictionaries or objects to the template just like lists or tuples. Then, within the template, you can access their properties using the appropriate syntax. For example, if each product was represented as a dictionary, you might access the name using {{ product.name }}. Another question is, "What happens if the database query returns no results?" You can use Jinja2's conditional statements to handle this case gracefully. For example, you could check if the products list is empty before iterating over it, and display a message like "No products found" if it is. Effectively combining database queries with HTML templates is crucial for building dynamic and data-driven web applications. It's the mechanism by which we bring data from the database to the user's screen, creating interactive and informative web experiences.

EXERCISE

Let's create a practical exercise to solidify our understanding of database interaction within a Flask application: building a simple CRUD (Create, Read, Update, Delete) web application. Imagine creating a basic to-do list application. We'll need a database table to store the tasks, and our web application will allow users to add new tasks, view existing tasks, and delete tasks. We'll use SQLite for this example due to its ease of setup, but the principles apply to other databases as well. First, we'll design our database table, perhaps named "tasks," with columns for id (primary key), description (the task itself), and completed (a boolean indicating whether the task is done).

In our Flask application, we'll define routes for each of the CRUD operations. The "Read" operation (viewing tasks) will involve fetching all tasks from the database and displaying them in a template. The "Create" operation (adding a task) will involve displaying a form where the user can enter a new task description. Upon form submission, we'll insert the new task into the database. The "Delete" operation will involve identifying the task to be deleted (perhaps through a hidden input field in the form) and then removing it from the database. For the "Update" operation, we can add a way to mark tasks as completed or edit their descriptions. This would involve fetching the task data, pre-filling an edit form, and then updating the database upon form submission.

A key challenge here is managing database connections. We want to ensure that connections are opened when needed and closed promptly to avoid resource leaks. One approach is to use Flask's g object to store the database connection, making it available throughout the request. We can create a function to establish the connection if it doesn't exist and close it at the end of the request. Another important aspect is preventing SQL injection vulnerabilities. We'll use parameterized queries for all database interactions, ensuring that user input is treated as data and not as executable SQL code. A common question is, "How do I handle errors during database operations?" We can use try...except blocks to catch potential exceptions, such as database connection errors or invalid SQL queries, and display appropriate error messages to the user. This exercise provides a hands-on experience in building a complete web application that interacts with a database, covering the essential aspects of CRUD operations, connection management, and security best practices. It serves as a solid foundation for developing more complex data-driven web applications.

CHAPTER 6

USER AUTHENTICATION

UNDERSTANDING AUTHENTICATION CONCEPTS

Authentication and authorization are two distinct but related concepts in web security. Authentication verifies *who* a user is, while authorization determines *what* a user is allowed to do. Think of it like a bouncer at a club. Authentication is like checking the ID to confirm the person is of legal age and a member (or not) of the club. Authorization is then deciding whether they get access to the VIP area, the backstage, or just the general dance floor. A user might be authenticated (their identity is confirmed), but they might not be authorized to access certain resources. For example, a user might be able to log in to an e-commerce site (authenticated), but they might not be authorized to access the admin panel (not authorized). This separation is crucial for security, ensuring that users only have access to the resources they are permitted to use.

Hashing passwords is paramount for protecting user credentials. Instead of storing passwords in plain text, which would be disastrous if the database were compromised, we store a *hash* of the password. A hash is a one-way function that transforms the password into a seemingly random string of characters. It's computationally infeasible to reverse the hash to get the original password. When a user tries to log in, we hash the password they enter and compare it to the stored hash. If the hashes match, we know the user entered the correct password, even though we never stored the actual password itself. Imagine a website storing user passwords in plain text; if a hacker gains access to the database, all user passwords would be exposed. However, if the passwords are hashed, the hacker would only get a bunch of seemingly meaningless strings.

A common question is, "Why not just encrypt the passwords instead of hashing them?" Encryption is a two-way process; you can encrypt data and then decrypt it back to the original value. While encrypting passwords might seem like a good idea, it introduces the risk of the encryption key being compromised. If the key is compromised, all the encrypted passwords could be decrypted. Hashing, being a one-way function, avoids this risk. Another question is, "What makes a good password hash?" A good password hash function should be computationally expensive to compute, making it difficult for attackers to crack the hashes using brute-force attacks. It should also be resistant to collision attacks, where two different passwords produce the same hash. Modern hashing algorithms like bcrypt and

Argon2 are designed to be computationally expensive and resistant to various attacks, making them suitable for password hashing (Provos & Mazieres, 2007). Using a strong hashing algorithm and properly salting the passwords (adding a unique random string to each password before hashing) are essential best practices for secure password storage.

IMPLEMENTING USER REGISTRATION

Securely storing user passwords in a database is paramount for protecting user privacy and preventing unauthorized access. Storing passwords in plain text is a catastrophic security vulnerability. Even encrypting passwords, while seemingly better, still poses a risk if the encryption key is compromised. The industry best practice is to *hash* passwords using a strong, one-way cryptographic hash function. This means transforming the password into an irreversible string of characters, the hash. When a user tries to log in, the entered password is hashed using the same algorithm, and the resulting hash is compared to the stored hash. If they match, the user is authenticated without ever needing to store the actual password.

Choosing the right hashing algorithm is crucial. Older algorithms like MD5 and SHA1 are now considered insecure due to their susceptibility to various attacks, including rainbow table attacks. Modern password hashing algorithms are designed to be computationally expensive, making brute-force attacks impractical. bcrypt and Argon2 are currently considered the strongest and most recommended password hashing algorithms (Bernstein, 2000). bcrypt is widely used and has been extensively analyzed, while Argon2 is a newer algorithm that offers even stronger resistance to various attacks, including side-channel attacks. When implementing user registration, you should *always* use bcrypt or Argon2 to hash passwords before storing them in the database.

A common question is, "Why are bcrypt and Argon2 considered better than other hashing algorithms?" These algorithms are specifically designed to be computationally expensive, meaning that it takes a significant amount of computing power to generate a hash. This makes brute-force attacks, where an attacker tries to guess passwords by generating hashes for millions of potential passwords, much less feasible. Furthermore, they are designed to be resistant to various other attacks, such as collision attacks and rainbow table attacks. Another crucial aspect of secure password storage is *salting*. Salting involves adding a unique random string to each password before hashing it. This makes it even more difficult for attackers to crack the hashes, even if they have access to a database of pre-computed hashes (rainbow tables). Each user should have their own unique salt. When a user registers, generate a random salt, store it along with the password hash, and then use that same salt when the user logs in to hash the entered password for comparison. In summary, implementing secure user registration requires using a strong password hashing algorithm like bcrypt or Argon2, salting each password uniquely, and never storing passwords in plain text. These practices are fundamental for protecting user credentials and maintaining the security of your web application.

USER LOGIN AND LOGOUT

Managing user sessions is crucial for maintaining user state and providing personalized experiences in web applications. Once a user is authenticated (their identity is verified), we need a way to track their activity and maintain their logged-in status as they navigate through different pages of the application. This is where sessions come into play. A session is essentially a server-side data store that is associated with a specific user. It allows us to store user-specific data, such as their username, preferences, or shopping cart items, without having to send this data back and forth between the client and the server on every request. Flask provides built-in support for sessions, typically using cookies to store a session ID on the client-side.

Cookies are small text files that websites store on a user's computer. They can be used for various purposes, including session management, storing user preferences, and tracking user activity. In the context of authentication, a cookie is often used to store a unique session ID. When a user logs in, the server generates a unique session ID, stores it in the session data store, and sends it to the client's browser as a cookie. The browser then automatically sends this cookie with every subsequent request to the server. The server can then use the session ID in the cookie to look up the corresponding session data in the data store, effectively maintaining the user's logged-in state. Imagine a user adding items to their shopping cart on an e-commerce site. The shopping cart data is stored in the user's session, associated with the session ID stored in the cookie. As the user navigates through the site, the server uses the cookie to retrieve the shopping cart data from the session, preserving the user's cart contents.

A common question is, "Are cookies secure?" While cookies themselves are not inherently insecure, they can be vulnerable to certain attacks, such as cross-site scripting (XSS) and cross-site request forgery (CSRF). To mitigate these risks, it's crucial to use secure cookies with appropriate attributes, such as HttpOnly and Secure. The HttpOnly attribute prevents JavaScript from accessing the cookie, mitigating XSS attacks. The Secure attribute ensures that the cookie is only transmitted over HTTPS, preventing interception by malicious parties. Another question is, "How long should sessions last?" The appropriate session duration depends on the application's requirements. Shorter session durations are more secure, as they limit the window of opportunity for attackers if a cookie is compromised. Longer session durations are more convenient for users, as they don't have to log in as frequently. A common approach is to use a combination of short-lived session cookies and longer-lived "remember me" cookies. When the user closes the browser, the short-lived session cookie is deleted, logging the user out. If the user selects "remember me," a longer-lived cookie is set, allowing the user to remain logged in even after closing the browser. However, "remember me" cookies should be used with caution, as they pose a greater security risk if the user's computer is compromised. Effectively managing user sessions and understanding the role of cookies are fundamental for building secure and user-friendly web applications.

SESSION MANAGEMENT WITH FLASK

Flask's session management system provides a convenient way to store user-specific data between requests, crucial for personalized web experiences. By default, Flask utilizes signed cookies to manage sessions. This means the session data is serialized, cryptographically signed, and then stored within a cookie on the client's browser. The signing mechanism ensures the cookie's integrity, preventing users from tampering with the session data. Upon receiving a request, Flask retrieves the session cookie, verifies the signature, and deserializes the data, making it accessible through the session object. This session object acts much like a Python dictionary, allowing you to store and retrieve data associated with the user's session. For instance, after a successful login, you might store the username: session['username'] = 'user123'. This data will be readily available across subsequent requests from that user.

While signed cookies are the default and often simplest approach, they do have limitations. Storing large amounts of data in cookies can impact performance due to increased data transfer. Also, cookies have size restrictions. More importantly, while the data is signed, storing highly sensitive information directly in cookies, even if encrypted, might not be the best practice for all applications. Flask offers the flexibility to configure alternative session storage mechanisms to overcome these limitations. You can opt for server-side session stores, such as storing session data in a database (like Redis or Memcached). With this approach, the cookie only stores a session ID, while the actual session data resides securely on the server. This enhances security and scalability. Implementing a server-side session store often involves using a Flask extension or creating a custom session interface.

A common question is, "How does Flask handle session expiration?" By default, Flask's session cookies expire when the user closes their browser. However, you can configure the session cookie's lifetime to persist sessions across browser closures, which is often implemented through a "remember me" feature. When a user selects "remember me" during login, a longer-lived cookie is set. This approach presents a trade-off: improved user convenience versus a slightly increased security risk if the user's machine is compromised. Another frequent question revolves around the security implications of using cookies for sessions. While signed cookies offer reasonable security, it's imperative to use secure cookie attributes like HttpOnly and Secure to further mitigate potential risks. The HttpOnly attribute blocks JavaScript access to the cookie, protecting against XSS attacks, while the Secure attribute ensures the cookie is only transmitted over HTTPS, preventing interception on insecure networks. Properly managing sessions in Flask, including selecting the right storage mechanism and using secure cookie attributes, is essential for building secure and user-friendly web applications.

USING FLASK-LOGIN

Flask-Login is a powerful extension that significantly simplifies user authentication management in Flask applications. It handles many of the common tasks associated with user login, logout, session management, and user object loading, allowing developers to focus on the core logic of their application rather than the intricacies of authentication. Imagine building a social media platform; you'd need to manage user accounts, track login status, and control access to different parts of the site. Without Flask-Login, you'd have to implement all of this yourself, which can be complex and error-prone. Flask-Login provides a standardized and well-tested way to handle these tasks, reducing development time and improving security.

One of the key features of Flask-Login is its ability to manage user sessions. It provides a convenient way to store and retrieve user objects from the session, making it easy to access user information throughout your application. It also handles the setting and clearing of session cookies, streamlining the login and logout process. Another important feature is its support for "remember me" functionality, allowing users to stay logged in even after closing their browser. Flask-

Login provides the necessary tools to implement this feature securely. Furthermore, it integrates seamlessly with Flask's view functions and templates, making it easy to protect specific routes or display user-specific information. For example, you can use the @login_required decorator to restrict access to certain routes to authenticated users only.

A common question is, "How does Flask-Login know how to load user information?" You are responsible for providing a user loader function that takes a user ID and returns the corresponding user object from your database. Flask-Login uses this function to retrieve user information from the database whenever it needs to access the currently logged-in user. This allows you to integrate Flask-Login with your existing database schema and user model. Another question is, "Does Flask-Login handle password hashing?" No, Flask-Login does *not* handle password hashing. It focuses on session management and user object loading. You are still responsible for securely hashing user passwords before storing them in the database, using a strong hashing algorithm like bcrypt or Argon2. Flask-Login simplifies the authentication workflow, but it's crucial to remember that secure password storage is still your responsibility. In summary, Flask-Login simplifies user authentication by providing tools for session management, "remember me" functionality, and easy integration with Flask's routing system. It reduces boilerplate code and promotes secure authentication practices, allowing developers to focus on building the core features of their web applications.

EXERCISE

Let's solidify our understanding of user authentication by outlining a practical exercise: implementing a complete user authentication system in a Flask application. Imagine building a simple forum or blog where users need to register and log in to post comments or create content. This exercise will cover user registration, login, and logout functionality, incorporating best practices for security. First, we'll design our database schema, including a "users" table with fields for username, email, password hash, and perhaps other relevant information. We'll use a strong password hashing algorithm like bcrypt or Argon2 to securely store user passwords. During registration, we'll hash the user's password before storing it in the database.

Next, we'll implement the registration form and view. The form will collect the user's information, and the view will handle form submission, validation, and database insertion. Crucially, we'll use parameterized queries to prevent SQL injection vulnerabilities. We'll also implement client-side validation to provide immediate feedback to the user. For the login functionality, we'll use Flask-Login to manage user sessions. We'll create a user loader function that retrieves user information from the database based on the user ID. Upon successful login, Flask-Login will create a user session, allowing the user to access protected routes. The logout functionality will simply clear the user session, effectively logging the user out.

A common challenge is integrating Flask-Login with our existing user model and database schema. The user loader function is key to this integration. It's responsible for fetching the user object from the database based on the user ID stored in the session. Another important consideration is handling different login scenarios, such as invalid credentials or account verification. We'll implement appropriate error handling and feedback mechanisms to guide the user through the login process. A crucial aspect of this exercise is security. We'll ensure that all sensitive operations, such as password hashing and session management, are handled securely. We'll also use HTTPS to protect user data during transmission. This exercise provides a hands-on experience in building a complete user authentication system, covering registration, login, logout, and security best practices. It serves as a solid foundation for building secure and user-friendly web applications that require authentication

and authorization.

CHAPTER 7

WORKING WITH STATIC

FILES

THE STATIC DIRECTORY

Organizing static files, such as CSS stylesheets, JavaScript files, images, and fonts, into a dedicated directory, typically named "static," is a standard practice in web development and highly recommended in Flask projects. This separation offers several key benefits that contribute to a more maintainable, efficient, and scalable web application. Imagine building a complex e-commerce website with numerous pages, each requiring various CSS and JavaScript files. Scattering these files throughout your project directory would quickly lead to chaos, making it difficult to locate, update, and manage them. The "static" directory provides a centralized location for all these assets, creating a clear and organized structure. This improved organization is particularly beneficial for larger projects with multiple developers, as it establishes a common understanding of where to find these resources.

Beyond organization, separating static files also improves performance. Web servers are often configured to serve static files directly without involving the Flask application. This is significantly faster, as the web server can handle these requests more efficiently than having Flask process them. Think of it like a restaurant having a separate area for storing pre-prepared ingredients; when an order comes in, the kitchen staff can quickly grab the ingredients they need without having to search through the entire restaurant. This optimization reduces the load on the Flask application, allowing it to handle more dynamic requests and improving overall website performance. Furthermore, separating static files makes deployment easier. You can configure your web server (like Nginx or Apache) to serve the "static" directory directly, independently of your Flask application. This allows you to scale your application more easily, as you can deploy your static files to a content delivery network (CDN) for faster global access without affecting your Flask application servers.

A common question is, "Why not just put all the static files in the same directory as my Flask application code?" While technically possible, this approach quickly becomes unwieldy as the project grows. Separating static files keeps the code directory clean and focused on the application logic, making it easier to understand and maintain. Another question is, "How does Flask know where to find the static files?" Flask, by default, looks for static files in a directory named "static" located in the same directory as your main Flask application file. You can customize this directory if needed, but the "static" convention is widely followed. In your templates, you can use the url_for('static', filename='style.css') function to generate the correct URL for your static files, ensuring that they are served correctly regardless of your deployment configuration. In summary, keeping static files in a separate directory promotes code organization, improves performance, simplifies deployment, and enhances scalability, making it a crucial practice for any serious web development project.

LINKING STATIC FILES IN TEMPLATES

Linking static files like CSS stylesheets, JavaScript files, and images in HTML templates is essential for creating visually appealing and interactive web applications. Flask, along with Jinja2, provides a clean and efficient way to manage these links. The key is to use the url_for() function within your templates. This function generates the correct URL for your static files, ensuring that they are served correctly regardless of your application's deployment configuration. Imagine you have a CSS file named style.css located in your "static" directory. Instead of hardcoding the path to this file in your HTML, you would use {{ url_for('static', filename='style.css') }} within your template. Jinja2 will then replace this expression with the actual URL to your style.css file. This approach is highly recommended because it makes your templates more portable and less prone to errors.

The url_for() function takes two main arguments: 'static' and filename. The 'static' argument indicates that you are linking a static file, and the filename argument specifies the name of the file you want to link. For example, to link a JavaScript file named script.js, you would use {{ url_for('static', filename='script.js') }}. For images, you would use the same approach: {{ url_for('static', filename='images/logo.png') }}. Notice that for images, you can specify subdirectories within the "static" directory. This allows you to organize your static files into logical groups, which is especially helpful for larger projects.

A common question is, "Why is using url_for() better than hardcoding the paths to my static files?" The main advantage is that url_for() generates URLs relative to your application's root, regardless of how your application is deployed. If you hardcode paths, they might break if you move your application to a different server or change the URL structure. url_for() handles this automatically, ensuring that your links always work correctly. Another question is, "Can I use query parameters with url_for() for static files?" Yes, you can. This can be useful for cache busting. You can append query parameters to the URL generated by url_for() to force browsers to download the latest version of a static file, even if it has been cached. For example: {{ url_for('static', filename='style.css', _v=1) }}. In summary, using url_for() to link static files in your Flask templates is a best practice that promotes portability, maintainability, and efficiency. It ensures that your static files are served correctly and simplifies the management of your web application's assets.

ORGANIZING STATIC FILE

Organizing static files effectively is crucial for maintaining a clean and scalable web application, especially as the project grows. A well-structured "static" directory not only improves developer experience but also contributes to efficient asset management and deployment. Imagine working on a large e-commerce platform with hundreds of images, stylesheets, and JavaScript files. A flat, unstructured "static" directory would quickly become a nightmare to navigate. Therefore, creating subdirectories within "static" is highly recommended. A common approach is to categorize files by type: css for stylesheets, js for JavaScript, img or images for images, and fonts for fonts. This simple categorization immediately improves organization, making it easier to locate specific files.

Beyond categorizing by file type, consider organizing files further based on functionality or page context. For example, you might have a product directory within img to store images specific to product pages, or a forms directory within css for styles related to forms. This contextual organization is particularly useful for larger projects with multiple developers, as it provides a clear understanding of which files are associated with which parts of the application. Think of a large social media platform; they might have separate directories for profile images, post images, and ad creatives, all within the img directory. This level of organization not only improves maintainability but also simplifies asset management and deployment.

A common question is, "How deep should I nest these subdirectories?" The depth of nesting depends on the complexity of your project. For smaller projects, a single level of categorization (by file type) might be sufficient. For larger projects, a second level of nesting (by context or functionality) can be beneficial. However, avoid excessive nesting, as it can make navigating the directory structure cumbersome. Another question is, "How do I reference these organized static files in my HTML templates?" You continue to use the url_for() function, but you include the subdirectory in the filename argument. For example, {{ url_for('static', filename='css/style.css') }} would link to a stylesheet located in the css subdirectory within the "static" directory. This approach ensures that your templates remain portable and that the links to your static files are generated correctly, regardless of your deployment configuration. Maintaining a well-organized "static" directory is an essential practice for building and maintaining scalable and manageable web applications. It improves collaboration, simplifies deployment, and contributes to the overall efficiency of the development process.

Using a CDN for Static Files

Using a Content Delivery Network (CDN) for static files is a crucial optimization technique for improving website performance and scalability, especially for applications with a global audience or high traffic. Imagine running a popular e-commerce website. Users from all over the world access your site, downloading images, CSS, and JavaScript files. If your server is located in a single location, users far from that server will experience slower loading times due to increased latency. A CDN solves this problem by storing copies of your static files on servers distributed geographically across the globe. When a user requests a static file, the CDN serves it from the server closest to the user, minimizing latency and significantly improving loading times.

The advantages of using a CDN are numerous. First and foremost is improved website performance. By reducing latency, CDNs make your website load faster, leading to a better user experience. This is particularly important for images and other large static assets. Second, CDNs reduce the load on your origin server. Since the CDN handles the serving of static files, your server can focus on processing dynamic requests, such as handling user logins or database queries. This frees up server resources and allows your application to handle more traffic. Third, CDNs improve website availability. If your origin server goes down, the CDN can still serve the static files, ensuring that your website remains partially functional. Fourth, CDNs can improve SEO. Search engines consider website loading speed as a ranking factor, so using a CDN can positively impact your search engine rankings. Think of a large news website; they often use CDNs to serve their images and videos, ensuring that users around the world can access the content quickly and reliably.

A common question is, "How do I integrate a CDN with my Flask application?" The process typically involves configuring your web server or using a CDN service's provided tools to upload your static files to the CDN. Once the files are on the CDN, you need to update the URLs in your HTML templates to point to the CDN's servers. This can be done manually or through configuration settings in your Flask application. Another question is, "What are the costs associated with using a CDN?" CDN providers typically charge based on the amount of data transferred. However, the performance benefits and reduced server load often outweigh the costs, especially for high-traffic websites. In summary, using a CDN for static files is a best practice for building scalable and performant web applications. It improves user experience, reduces server load, increases website availability, and can even positively impact SEO.

EXERCISE

Let's enhance our user authentication system with styling and interactivity, bringing it closer to a polished web application. This exercise focuses on integrating CSS for visual presentation and adding JavaScript for dynamic behavior. Imagine we're refining our earlier to-do list application with user authentication; we'll want to make it visually appealing and perhaps add some interactive elements. First, we'll create a CSS stylesheet, perhaps named style.css, within our "static/css" directory. This stylesheet will contain the CSS rules to style our HTML elements, controlling the layout, colors, fonts, and overall appearance of our application. We'll define styles for the forms, buttons, error messages, and any other elements we want to customize. For example, we might style the login form to have a clean and modern look, or we might add hover effects to the buttons to provide visual feedback to the user.

Next, we'll link this stylesheet to our HTML templates using the url_for() function, as discussed previously. This ensures that the styles are applied correctly to all pages. We can then start styling our application, making it more user-friendly and visually appealing.

Beyond styling, we'll add some interactive JavaScript functionality. Perhaps we want to add a "live search" feature to our to-do list, where users can start typing a task description and see matching tasks appear in real-time. We'll create a JavaScript file, perhaps named script.js, within our "static/js" directory, and write the JavaScript code to implement this functionality. This might involve listening for keyboard input, making AJAX requests to the server to fetch matching tasks, and updating the HTML dynamically. We might also use JavaScript to handle form validation on the client-side, providing immediate feedback to the user if they enter invalid data.

A common challenge is ensuring that the JavaScript code interacts correctly with the server-side logic. We might need to send data to the server, receive data from the server, or trigger server-side actions. This often involves using AJAX (Asynchronous JavaScript and XML) or Fetch API calls to communicate with the server. Another important aspect is ensuring that the JavaScript code is well-organized and maintainable. We can use modular JavaScript techniques or frameworks like jQuery to structure our code effectively. A key point to consider is the separation of concerns. We want to keep the HTML focused on structure, the CSS focused on presentation, and the

JavaScript focused on behavior. This separation makes our code more maintainable and easier to understand. This exercise provides a practical experience in integrating CSS and JavaScript into a Flask application, enhancing both the visual appeal and the interactivity of the application. It demonstrates how to combine frontend technologies with backend logic to create a more complete and engaging user experience.

CHAPTER 8

API DEVELOPMENT

WITH FLASK

WHAT ARE APIS?

APIs, or Application Programming Interfaces, are essential building blocks of modern software systems, enabling different applications to communicate and exchange data with each other. Think of them as intermediaries that define how different software components can interact, regardless of their underlying technologies. Imagine a mobile app that needs to display data from a website. Instead of directly accessing the website's database, the app can use an API provided by the website to request and receive the necessary data in a structured format, such as JSON. This separation of concerns allows the website to evolve its data storage without affecting the mobile app, as long as the API remains consistent.

The benefits of using APIs are numerous. They promote code reusability, as different applications can use the same API to access data or functionality. They enable interoperability, allowing applications written in different programming languages and running on different platforms to communicate seamlessly. They facilitate modularity, as applications can be built as a collection of interconnected services, each exposing its functionality through an

API. They also foster innovation, as third-party developers can use APIs to build new applications or services that integrate with existing ones. For example, a mapping service might provide an API that allows other applications to embed maps or access location data.

- RESTful principles are a set of guidelines for designing APIs that are scalable, maintainable, and easy to understand. REST (Representational State Transfer) is an architectural style that emphasizes the use of standard HTTP methods (GET, POST, PUT, DELETE) to interact with resources, which are identified by URLs. RESTful APIs typically use lightweight data formats like JSON or XML to exchange data. Key principles of REST include statelessness, meaning that each request from the client to the server must contain all the information needed to understand and process the request; cacheability, allowing responses to be cached to improve performance; and a uniform interface, using consistent conventions for naming resources and defining operations. A well-designed RESTful API is self-documenting to a large extent, making it easier for developers to understand and use. For example, a RESTful API for a library might use /books to represent the collection of books, /books/123 to represent a specific book with ID 123, and use GET requests to retrieve book information, POST requests to add new books, PUT requests to update book information, and DELETE requests to remove books. Adhering to RESTful principles leads to APIs that are robust, scalable, and easy to integrate with, which are essential for building modern web applications.

CREATING API ENDPOINTS

Defining API endpoints in Flask is remarkably similar to defining web page routes, leveraging the familiar @app.route decorator. However, instead of returning HTML to be rendered in a browser, API endpoints typically return data in a format like JSON, which can be easily consumed by other applications. Imagine building an API for a task management application. You might want an endpoint /tasks to retrieve a list of tasks and another endpoint /tasks/123 to retrieve a specific task with ID 123. In Flask, you would define these endpoints using the @app.route decorator, just like you would for regular web pages. For example: @app.route('/tasks', methods=['GET']) would define an endpoint that handles GET requests to /tasks. Inside the associated function, you would fetch the list of tasks from your database and return them as a JSON response using jsonify().

The methods argument in the @app.route decorator is crucial for specifying which HTTP methods an endpoint should handle. RESTful APIs utilize different HTTP methods to perform different actions on resources. GET is typically used for retrieving data, POST for creating new resources, PUT for updating existing resources, and DELETE for removing resources. For example, if you wanted to create a new task, you would use a POST request to the /tasks endpoint. You would define this endpoint as @app.route('/tasks', methods=['POST']). Inside the function, you would access the data submitted in the request body (typically in JSON format), create a new task in your database, and return a success response, perhaps including the ID of the newly created task. Similarly, you would use PUT to update a task (e.g., @app.route('/tasks/<int:task_id>', methods=['PUT'])) and DELETE to remove a task (e.g., @app.route('/tasks/<int:task_id>', methods=['DELETE']). The <int:task_id> part of the route definition allows you to capture a parameter from the URL, which can be useful for identifying specific resources.

A common question is, "How do I handle different HTTP methods for the same URL?" You simply include all the desired methods in the methods argument. For example, if you wanted an endpoint to handle both GET (to retrieve a task) and PUT (to update a task) requests to the same URL, you would define it as @app.route('/tasks/<int:task_id>', methods=['GET', 'PUT']). Another question is, "How do I return JSON responses from my API endpoints?" Flask provides the jsonify() function, which automatically converts Python dictionaries and lists into JSON responses. This makes it easy to return structured data from your API endpoints. For example, return jsonify({'message': 'Task created successfully', 'task_id': 123}), 201 would return a JSON response with a success message and a task ID, along with a 201 status code (Created). Properly defining API endpoints and using the appropriate HTTP methods are fundamental for building RESTful APIs that are scalable, maintainable, and easy to integrate with.

HANDLING JSON DATA

Handling JSON data is fundamental to building modern web APIs, as it's the most common format for data exchange between client and server. In Flask, working with JSON data involves two key processes: serialization (converting Python objects to JSON) and deserialization (converting JSON data to Python objects). Imagine building an API for a social media platform. When a user creates a new post, the client application sends the post data to the server in JSON format. The server then deserializes this JSON data into Python objects, allowing it to be processed and stored in the database. Later, when the client requests to view the post, the server serializes the post data from the database (which is in Python object form) back into JSON format and sends it as the API response.

Flask simplifies JSON serialization using the jsonify() function. This function takes a Python dictionary or list and automatically converts it into a JSON response with the correct Content-Type header (application/json). For example, if you have a Python dictionary representing a user, you can serialize it like this: return jsonify({'username': 'john_doe', 'email': 'john.doe@example.com'}). Flask handles the conversion to JSON and sets the appropriate headers. For deserialization, Flask provides the request.get_json() method. This method parses the incoming JSON data from the request body and converts it into a Python dictionary. For instance, if the client sends JSON data representing a new product, you can access this data in your Flask view using product_data = request.get_json(). You can then access the individual product attributes using dictionary keys, like product_data['name'] or product_data['price'].

A common question is, "What happens if the client sends invalid JSON data?" request.get_json() will return None if the request body does not contain valid JSON. It's crucial to handle this case gracefully in your code to prevent errors. You can check if request.get_json() returns None and return an appropriate error response to the client if necessary. Another question is, "How can I handle more complex Python objects, like custom classes, during JSON serialization?" The default jsonify() function can handle basic Python data types. For more complex objects, you might need to convert them to dictionaries first or use a more advanced JSON library like simplejson or marshmallow, which provide more control over the serialization process. Properly handling JSON data serialization and deserialization is essential for building robust and interoperable web APIs. It ensures that your API can communicate effectively with clients and exchange data in a standardized and easily consumable format.

API Authentication

Securing APIs is paramount to protecting sensitive data and preventing unauthorized access. Without proper authentication and authorization, APIs can become vulnerable to various attacks, potentially exposing valuable information or allowing malicious actors to manipulate data. Several methods exist for securing APIs, each with its own strengths and weaknesses. API keys are a simple form of authentication often used for less sensitive APIs. They are essentially unique identifiers assigned to each API consumer. When a request is made to the API, the API key is included in the request, typically in a header or as a query parameter. The API server then verifies the key against a list of valid keys. Think of it like a membership card; possessing a valid card grants you access. However, API keys alone are not sufficient for highly sensitive data, as they can be easily intercepted or shared.

OAuth (Open Authorization) is a more robust authorization framework that allows third-party applications to access resources on behalf of a user without sharing the user's credentials. Imagine using a third-party app to access your photos on a social media platform.

OAuth allows the app to request access to your photos without ever knowing your social media password. It works through a process of token exchange. The user grants permission to the third-party app to access their resources, and the app receives an access token. This token is then used by the app to make requests to the API. OAuth provides a more secure way to grant access to resources, as it doesn't involve sharing user credentials directly. There are different versions of OAuth, with OAuth 2.0 being the most widely used.

A common question is, "When should I use API keys vs. OAuth?" API keys are suitable for simpler APIs where the risk of unauthorized access is relatively low. They are easy to implement and manage. OAuth is recommended for APIs that handle sensitive data or require fine-grained control over access permissions. For example, a financial API should definitely use OAuth to protect user financial information. Another question is, "Are there other API authentication methods besides API keys and OAuth?" Yes, there are other methods, such as Basic Authentication (using username and password), Digest Authentication, and JWT (JSON Web Tokens). Each method has its own use cases and security implications. JWT, for example, is often used in conjunction with OAuth to provide a more secure and efficient way to manage access tokens. Choosing the right API authentication method depends on the sensitivity of the data, the complexity of the authorization requirements, and the specific needs of your application. Properly securing your APIs is crucial for protecting your data and ensuring the integrity of your application.

TESTING APIs

Testing APIs is a crucial step in the development process, ensuring they function correctly and meet the desired specifications. Thorough testing helps identify bugs early, prevents unexpected behavior in production, and ultimately leads to more reliable and robust APIs. Several approaches can be used to test APIs, ranging from simple manual testing using tools like curl or Postman to more sophisticated automated testing using frameworks like pytest or requests. Imagine building an API for an online bookstore. You would want to test various scenarios, such as retrieving book information, adding a book to the catalog, updating book details, or deleting a book. Each of these scenarios represents a test case that needs to be verified.

Manual testing using tools like Postman allows you to send HTTP requests to your API endpoints and inspect the responses. This is useful for quickly testing individual endpoints and exploring the API's behavior. However, manual testing is not scalable for large APIs with many endpoints and complex interactions. Automated testing, on the other hand, allows you to define test cases programmatically and run them repeatedly. This is essential for continuous integration and continuous deployment (CI/CD) pipelines, where tests are run automatically with every code change. For example, you could use pytest and the requests library to write Python code that sends different types of requests to your API endpoints and asserts that the responses are as expected. You might test for correct status codes, valid JSON responses, and proper data handling.

A common question is, "What should I test in my API?" You should test all aspects of your API, including: correct routing (ensuring requests are routed to the correct handler), proper HTTP methods (verifying that endpoints handle the correct HTTP methods), data validation (checking if the API handles invalid input gracefully), authentication and authorization (testing if access controls are working as expected), and error handling (ensuring the API returns appropriate error responses). Another important aspect of API testing is documentation. Tools like Swagger or OpenAPI allow you to define your API's structure and behavior in a standardized way, which can then be used to generate interactive documentation and automated tests. This not only helps developers understand and use your API but also makes testing more efficient. A good API testing strategy should include a combination of manual and automated testing, covering all aspects of the API's functionality and adhering to documentation standards. This ensures that your API is reliable, secure, and meets the needs of its consumers.

EXERCISE

Let's solidify our understanding of API development with Flask by outlining a practical exercise: building RESTful API for managing a simple data resource. Imagine creating an API for a task management application. We'll design this API to allow users to create new tasks, retrieve existing tasks, update task details, and delete tasks. This exercise will cover the core principles of RESTful API design, including proper use of HTTP methods and JSON data handling.

First, we'll define the API endpoints and their corresponding HTTP methods. For example, /tasks will handle GET requests to retrieve a list of tasks and POST requests to create a new task. /tasks/<int:task_id> will handle GET requests to retrieve a specific task, PUT requests to update a task, and DELETE requests to delete a task.

Next, we'll implement these endpoints in our Flask application. For GET requests to /tasks, we'll fetch the list of tasks from a data store (which could be a database, a list in memory, or a file) and return it as a JSON response using jsonify(). For POST requests to /tasks, we'll parse the JSON data from the request body using request.get_json(), create a new task in our data store, and return a success response, perhaps including the ID of the newly created task. For GET requests to /tasks/<int:task_id>, we'll retrieve the specific task from the data store based on the task_id and return it as a JSON response. For PUT requests, we'll parse the JSON data from the request body, update the corresponding task in the data store, and return a success response. For DELETE requests, we'll remove the task from the data store and return a success response.

A common challenge is handling different HTTP methods for the same URL. Flask's @app.route decorator with the methods argument makes this straightforward. We simply specify all the allowed methods in the methods argument. Another important consideration is error handling. We'll implement proper error handling to gracefully handle invalid requests, missing data, and other potential issues. We'll return appropriate HTTP status codes and error messages to the client. A crucial aspect of this exercise is adhering to RESTful principles. We'll use the correct HTTP methods for each operation, use meaningful resource names, and return appropriate status codes. This exercise provides a hands-on experience in building a complete RESTful API, covering the essential aspects of endpoint definition, JSON data handling, and RESTful principles. It serves as a solid foundation for developing more complex APIs that interact with databases and other services.

PART III

ADVANCED TOPICS AND

DEPLOYMENT

CHAPTER 9

TESTING YOUR FLASK

APPLICATIONS

WHY TESTING IS IMPORTANT

Testing is an absolutely crucial aspect of software development, and web applications are no exception. Writing tests for your Flask applications offers a multitude of benefits, ultimately leading to more robust, reliable, and maintainable software. Imagine building a complex e-commerce platform. Without thorough testing, a seemingly small change in one part of the code could inadvertently break functionality in another, leading to frustrated users, lost sales, and potentially even security vulnerabilities. Testing acts as a safety net, catching these regressions before they make it to production and impact your users. It allows you to confidently make changes to your code, knowing that the tests will alert you if anything unexpected breaks.

Beyond preventing regressions, testing also improves code quality. The act of writing tests forces you to think about your code from different perspectives, often revealing design flaws or edge cases you might have overlooked. It encourages you to write more modular and testable code, which in turn makes your application easier to understand and maintain. Think of it like building a house; you wouldn't just start putting up walls without first testing the foundation and ensuring it's solid. Similarly, you shouldn't deploy a web application without thoroughly testing its different components. Testing also facilitates collaboration. Well-written tests serve as documentation, clearly demonstrating how different parts of the application are supposed to work. This makes it easier for other developers to understand your code and contribute to the project.

A common question is, "When should I write tests?" The answer is: as early and as often as possible. Ideally, you should write tests *before* you write the code, following a practice known as Test-Driven Development (TDD). This approach helps you clarify your requirements and design your code for testability from the start. However, even if you're not following TDD, it's never too late to start writing tests. Another question is, "What should I test?" You should aim to test all critical parts of your application, including routes, views, models, forms, and API endpoints. Test for both positive cases (valid input, expected output) and negative cases (invalid input, error handling). Consider edge cases and boundary conditions. A good testing strategy involves a combination of unit tests (testing individual components in isolation), integration tests (testing how different components interact), and end-to-end tests (testing the entire application flow). Investing time in writing tests is an investment in the long-term quality and stability of your web application. It reduces the risk of bugs, improves code maintainability, and ultimately saves you time and effort in the long run.

Unit Testing

Unit testing is a fundamental practice in software development that involves testing individual units or components of an application in isolation. A "unit" can be a function, a class, a module, or any small, testable piece of code. The goal of unit testing is to verify that each unit is working correctly and as expected, independent of other units. Think of it like testing the individual parts of a car engine before assembling the entire engine. You want to make sure each piston, valve, and spark plug is functioning properly before putting them all together. In the context of Flask applications, unit tests might focus on testing specific functions in your views, models, or helper modules. For example, you might write a unit test to verify that a function that calculates the total price of items in a shopping cart is working correctly for different inputs.

Writing unit tests for Flask code typically involves using a testing framework like pytest or unittest. These frameworks provide tools for writing test functions, asserting expected outcomes, and running tests. Let's consider an example of testing a Flask view function that handles user login. You might write a unit test that simulates a user submitting valid login credentials and asserts that the view function returns a successful response (e.g., a redirect to the user's profile page). You would also write tests for negative cases, such as invalid credentials or missing input, asserting that the view function returns an appropriate error response. When writing unit tests, it's crucial to isolate the unit under test from any external dependencies, such as databases or APIs. This is often achieved using mocking or stubbing techniques. Mocking involves replacing a real dependency with a mock object that simulates the behavior of the real dependency. For example, you might mock the database connection in your unit tests to avoid actually interacting with the database during testing.

A common question is, "How do I test Flask views that interact with templates?" You can use Flask's test client to simulate requests to your Flask views and then inspect the response data. You can check the status code, the content of the response, and even the rendered template variables. However, it's generally recommended to keep unit tests focused on the logic within the view function and to avoid testing the template rendering itself. Template testing is often better handled through integration or end-to-end tests. Another question is, "How do I organize my unit tests?" It's a good practice to organize your unit tests in a directory structure that mirrors your application code. For example, if you have a module named users.py, you might have a corresponding test file named test_users.py in a "tests" directory. Following a consistent naming convention and directory structure makes it easier to find and run your unit tests. Unit testing is an essential practice for writing robust and maintainable Flask applications. It helps catch bugs early, improves code quality, and facilitates collaboration.

TESTING ROUTES AND VIEWS

Testing Flask routes and view functions is a critical part of ensuring the correct behavior of your web application. It verifies that your application handles requests correctly, returns the expected responses, and interacts with other parts of your application as intended. Think of it like testing the roads and intersections of a city's transportation system; you want to ensure that traffic flows smoothly and that drivers can reach their destinations without issues. In Flask, testing routes and views typically involves using Flask's built-in test client, which allows you to simulate HTTP requests to your application without actually starting a live server. This makes testing fast and efficient.

Using the test client, you can send various types of requests (GET, POST, PUT, DELETE) to your routes and then inspect the responses. You can check the status code, the response content, the headers, and even the data stored in the session. For example, imagine testing a route that handles user login. You might simulate a POST request to the login route with valid credentials and assert that the response is a redirect to the user's profile page (status code 302) and that the user's ID is stored in the session. You would also test the scenario where the user submits invalid credentials, asserting that the response is a 401 Unauthorized error or that an appropriate error message is displayed. Furthermore, you can test how your views interact with templates by checking if the correct template is rendered and if the expected variables are passed to the template.

A common question is, "How do I test routes that require authentication?" Flask-Login provides utilities for simulating logged-in users during testing. You can use the login_user() function within your tests to log in a user programmatically, allowing you to test routes that are protected by the @login_required decorator. Another question is, "How do I test views that interact with a database?" It's crucial to isolate your tests from the actual database to avoid dependencies and ensure that your tests are fast and reliable. You can achieve this using mocking or dependency injection. Mocking involves replacing the database connection or query functions with mock objects that simulate the behavior of the real database. Dependency injection involves passing the database connection or query functions as arguments to your views, making it easier to inject mock objects during testing. Thoroughly testing your Flask routes and views is crucial for building robust and reliable web applications. It ensures that your application handles requests correctly, interacts with other components as expected, and provides a consistent user experience.

TEST-DRIVEN DEVELOPMENT (TDD)

Test-Driven Development (TDD) is a software development methodology that emphasizes writing tests *before* writing the code they are intended to test. This approach might seem counterintuitive at first, but it offers significant benefits in terms of code quality, maintainability, and overall development efficiency. Imagine building a complex web application; starting with the tests forces you to clearly define what you expect your code to do *before* you actually implement it. This clarity helps prevent ambiguity and ensures that you are building the right thing from the start. TDD follows a simple, iterative cycle: Red, Green, Refactor. "Red" refers to writing a test that initially fails because the code it tests doesn't exist yet. "Green" refers to writing the minimal amount of code necessary to make the test pass. "Refactor" refers to improving the code's structure and design while ensuring that all tests still pass. This cycle repeats for each small unit of functionality, gradually building up the application, always guided by the tests.

Applying TDD to Flask applications involves writing tests for your routes, views, models, and other components *before* implementing them. For example, if you are about to implement a new API endpoint, you would first write a test that defines the expected behavior of that endpoint. This test might check the HTTP status code, the JSON response, and any other relevant aspects of the endpoint's output. Initially, this test will fail because the endpoint doesn't exist. You would then write the minimal amount of code necessary to make the test pass. This might involve creating the route, the view function, and any necessary data access logic. Once the test passes, you can then refactor the code, improving its structure, readability, and performance, while ensuring that the test continues to pass.

A common question is, "How do I decide what to test first when using TDD?" A good approach is to start with the most critical or core functionality of your application. Focus on the parts of the code that are most likely to have an impact if they are broken. Another question is, "What happens if my tests fail after I refactor my code?" If your tests fail after refactoring, it means you have inadvertently introduced a bug. This is one of the key benefits of TDD; the tests act as a safety net, catching regressions early. You can then fix the bug and ensure that all tests pass again. TDD promotes a disciplined and iterative development process, leading to code that is more robust, testable, and maintainable. While it might require a shift in mindset initially, the long-term benefits of TDD make it a valuable practice for any software developer.

EXERCISE

Let's put our understanding of testing into practice with a concrete exercise: writing unit tests for a Flask application. Imagine we have a simple Flask app with a few routes and view functions, perhaps including the user authentication system we developed earlier. Our goal is to write unit tests that cover the core functionality of these routes and views, ensuring they behave as expected. We'll use pytest for this exercise, a popular and powerful testing framework for Python. First, we'll create a "tests" directory in our project, where we'll store our test files. Each test file will typically correspond to a module or component in our application. For example, if we have a users.py module containing user-related functions, we might create a test_users.py file in the "tests" directory to hold the tests for those functions.

Within each test file, we'll define test functions, each focusing on testing a specific unit of functionality. For example, we might have a test function to verify the user registration process, checking that the user is created correctly in the database and that the appropriate response is returned. We might have another test function to check the login functionality, ensuring that valid credentials are accepted and invalid credentials are rejected. We'll use pytest's assertion mechanisms to verify the expected outcomes. For instance, we might assert that the response status code is 200 for a successful request or that a specific error message is present in the response. Crucially, we'll isolate our tests from external dependencies, like the database. We'll use mocking to replace the database interaction functions with mock objects that simulate the database's behavior. This ensures that our tests are fast, reliable, and independent of the actual database.

A common challenge is testing routes that require authentication. We can use Flask-Login's utilities to simulate logged-in users during testing. We can programmatically log in a user before making a request to a protected route, allowing us to test the route's behavior for authenticated users. Another important consideration is organizing our tests effectively. We'll follow a consistent naming convention for our test files and functions, making it easy to understand what each test covers. We'll also group related tests together using pytest's fixtures, which allow us to set up common test data or resources. This exercise provides a hands-on experience in writing unit tests for a Flask application, covering various aspects of testing routes, views, and authentication functionality. It reinforces the importance of testing in building robust and maintainable web applications.

CHAPTER 10

DEBUGGING AND ERROR

HANDLING

DEBUGGING TECHNIQUES

Debugging is an essential skill for any software developer, and Flask provides helpful tools to streamline the process. The built-in Flask debugger, when enabled (usually by setting debug=True), offers several advantages during development. When an error occurs, instead of a generic error message, you'll often see a detailed traceback in your browser, pinpointing the exact line of code causing the problem. This makes it significantly easier to identify the source of the error. Furthermore, the debugger often provides an interactive console where you can inspect variables and execute code in the context of the error, allowing you to experiment and understand the state of your application when the error occurred. Imagine developing a complex form submission process; if a validation error occurs, the debugger helps you inspect the submitted data, the validation logic, and the error messages, quickly revealing where the issue lies.

Beyond the Flask debugger, several other debugging techniques are valuable. print() statements, while seemingly simple, can be surprisingly effective for tracking the flow of execution and inspecting variable values at different points in your code. Logging, using Python's logging module, provides a more structured and persistent way to record information about your application's behavior. Logs can be invaluable for diagnosing issues in production environments where you don't have access to the interactive debugger. Debuggers like pdb (Python Debugger) offer more advanced features, allowing you to set breakpoints, step through code line by line, inspect variables, and even modify the execution flow. These are particularly helpful for complex bugs that are difficult to reproduce or understand with simpler techniques. Profiling tools can help identify performance bottlenecks in your application. They analyze your code's execution and pinpoint areas where it's spending excessive time, allowing you to optimize those sections.

A common question is, "When should I use the Flask debugger vs. other debugging techniques?" The Flask debugger is most useful during development for quickly identifying and fixing errors. print() statements are useful for simple debugging tasks or when you need to quickly inspect variable values. Logging is essential for debugging in production environments and for tracking the application's behavior over time. Debuggers like pdb are helpful for complex bugs that require more in-depth analysis. Profiling tools are crucial for optimizing performance. Another question is, "How can I effectively use logging in my Flask application?" Configure the logging module to write logs to a file, use different log levels (DEBUG, INFO, WARNING, ERROR, CRITICAL) to categorize log messages, and include relevant context information in your logs, such as timestamps, user IDs, or request details. Mastering different debugging techniques and choosing the right tool for the job is essential for any web developer, enabling you to efficiently identify and resolve issues in your Flask applications.

HANDLING ERRORS

Handling errors gracefully is crucial for creating robust and user-friendly web applications. When unexpected issues occur, such as database connection problems, invalid user input, or internal server errors, you want to handle them in a way that doesn't crash your application and provides informative feedback to the user. In Flask, you can handle errors using try...except blocks, just like in regular Python code. You can wrap the code that might raise an exception within a try block and then define except blocks to handle specific exceptions. For example, if you're interacting with a database, you might have a try block that attempts to execute a database query and an except block to handle OperationalError exceptions that might occur if the database connection is lost. Within the except block, you can log the error, display a user-friendly message, or take other appropriate actions.

However, simply catching exceptions is not enough. You also want to provide informative feedback to the user. Displaying raw error messages to users is generally a bad practice, as it can expose sensitive information about your application's internals. Instead, you should display custom error pages that are user-friendly and informative, guiding the user on what to do next. Flask makes it easy to define custom error handlers for different HTTP status codes. You can use the @app.errorhandler decorator to define a function that will be executed when a specific error occurs. For example, @app.errorhandler(404) would define a handler for "Page Not Found" errors. Within the error handler function, you can return a custom HTML template that displays a user-friendly 404 message. You can also pass relevant information to the template, such as a link back to the home page.

A common question is, "How can I handle different types of errors differently?" You can define multiple except blocks within a try block to handle different exceptions. You can also use the else block to specify code that should be executed only if no exceptions occur. Furthermore, you can define custom exception classes to represent specific errors in your application. This allows you to handle these errors more specifically. Another question is, "How can I log errors for debugging and monitoring?" You should use Python's logging module to log errors. This allows you to record detailed information about the error, including the traceback, the timestamp, and any other relevant context. Logging is crucial for debugging issues in production and for monitoring the health of your application. Implementing proper error handling and displaying custom error pages are essential for building robust and user-friendly Flask applications. They prevent your application from crashing, provide informative feedback to users, and help you diagnose and fix issues more efficiently.

LOGGING BEST PRACTICES

Logging is an indispensable practice in software development, particularly for web applications. It provides a detailed record of your application's behavior, allowing you to track events, diagnose errors, monitor performance, and gain valuable insights into how your application is being used. Imagine trying to debug a complex issue in a production environment without any logs; it would be like trying to find a needle in a haystack. Logging provides the breadcrumbs you need to retrace the steps leading to the problem. It's also crucial for security auditing, allowing you to track user activity and identify potential security breaches. Furthermore, logs can be used for performance analysis, helping you identify bottlenecks and optimize your application.

Several best practices should be followed for effective logging in Flask. First, use a logging library, like Python's built-in logging module. This provides a structured and flexible way to manage logs. Second, configure your logging to write logs to a file. This makes the logs persistent and allows you to analyze them even after the application has been restarted. Third, use different log levels (DEBUG, INFO,

WARNING, ERROR, CRITICAL) to categorize log messages. This allows you to filter logs based on their severity, focusing on the most important messages. Fourth, include relevant context information in your logs, such as timestamps, user IDs, request details, and any other information that might be helpful for debugging. For example, when logging an error, include the full traceback to pinpoint the exact location of the error.

A common question is, "How do I configure logging in a Flask application?" You can configure the logging module in your Flask application's entry point. You can specify the log file, the log format, and the minimum log level to capture. It's often a good idea to use environment variables to configure logging, allowing you to easily change the logging settings for different environments (development, production, etc.). Another question is, "How do I handle sensitive information in logs?" Avoid logging sensitive data, such as passwords, credit card numbers, or personal information. If you must log sensitive data, consider masking or redacting it before it's written to the log file. Furthermore, ensure that your log files are protected with appropriate file permissions to prevent unauthorized access. Following logging best practices is essential for building robust, maintainable, and secure Flask applications. It provides the information you need to debug issues, monitor performance, and ensure the smooth operation of your application.

EXERCISE

Let's solidify our understanding of debugging, error handling, and logging with a practical exercise: debugging a sample Flask application and implementing robust error handling and logging. Imagine we have a Flask application with a few routes, a database connection, and some form handling logic. However, the application contains several errors, such as incorrect database queries, unhandled exceptions, and missing input validation. Our goal is to identify and fix these errors, implement proper error handling to prevent the application from crashing, and add logging to track the application's behavior and assist in future debugging.

First, we'll run the Flask application with the debugger enabled (debug=True). This will allow us to see detailed tracebacks when errors occur, helping us pinpoint the location of the bugs. We'll systematically interact with the application, triggering different routes and functionalities, looking for error messages or unexpected behavior. When we encounter an error, we'll carefully examine the traceback, identify the root cause, and fix the code. For example, if we encounter a TypeError when trying to access a database field, we might realize that we're trying to access a field that doesn't exist or that the data type is incorrect. We'll correct the database query or adjust the code to handle the data type appropriately.

Next, we'll implement proper error handling using try...except blocks. We'll wrap potentially error-prone code, such as database interactions or form validation, within try blocks and define except blocks to handle specific exceptions. Within the except blocks, we'll log the error using Python's logging module and return a user-friendly error message or redirect to an error page. We'll also implement custom error handlers using Flask's @app.errorhandler decorator to handle specific HTTP errors, such as 404 Not Found or 500 Internal Server Error. Finally, we'll configure logging to write logs to a file, using different log levels to categorize log messages and including relevant context information, such as timestamps and user IDs. This exercise provides hands-on experience in debugging a Flask application, implementing robust error handling, and setting up effective logging. It reinforces the importance of these practices in building reliable and maintainable web applications.

CHAPTER 11

DEPLOYMENT

CHOOSING A DEPLOYMENT PLATFORM

Deploying a Flask application involves making it accessible to users over the internet. Several deployment platforms cater to varying needs and project scales, each with its own set of advantages and disadvantages. Choosing the right platform depends on factors like cost, scalability, control, and ease of use. One common option is deploying to a Platform as a Service (PaaS) provider like Heroku, PythonAnywhere, or Google App Engine. PaaS platforms abstract away much of the infrastructure management, allowing developers to focus primarily on the application code. They typically offer easy deployment processes, automatic scaling, and built-in support for common web application components. Imagine building a small to medium-sized web application; a PaaS provider might be an ideal choice due to its simplicity and ease of use. However, PaaS platforms can sometimes be more expensive than other options for larger applications and might offer less control over the underlying infrastructure.

Another option is deploying to an Infrastructure as a Service (IaaS) provider like Amazon Web Services (AWS), Google Cloud Platform (GCP), or Microsoft Azure. IaaS provides virtual servers that you have full control over. This offers greater flexibility and customization, allowing you to configure the server environment exactly as needed. IaaS is often preferred for larger applications with complex requirements or when fine-grained control over the infrastructure is essential. Think of deploying a large-scale e-commerce platform; IaaS provides the control and scalability needed to manage such a complex application. However, IaaS requires more technical expertise, as you are responsible for server setup, maintenance, and security. You also need to handle scaling yourself, which can be more complex than with PaaS.

A third option, often used for experimentation or very small projects, is deploying directly to a Virtual Private Server (VPS). A VPS gives you more control than shared hosting but less than IaaS. You are still responsible for server maintenance, but it can be a cost-effective solution for smaller projects that require some level of customization. Finally, for very simple applications, shared hosting might be an option, but it is generally not recommended for Flask applications due to its limitations and lack of control. A common question is, "Which platform should I choose?" There's no single answer. For small to medium-sized applications where ease of use and speed of deployment are priorities, a PaaS platform is a good choice. For larger, more complex applications requiring greater control and scalability, IaaS is often preferred. VPS offers a middle ground for smaller projects needing some customization. Consider your project's specific needs, your technical expertise, and your budget when making this decision.

PREPARING YOUR APPLICATION FOR DEPLOYMENT

Preparing your Flask application for deployment involves several key steps to ensure it runs smoothly in a production environment. Two important files often used in this process are the Procfile and requirements.txt. The Procfile is a simple text file that specifies the commands that your application server should execute to start your web application. Think of it as a set of instructions for the deployment platform. For example, if you're deploying to Heroku, your Procfile might contain a line like web: gunicorn app:app, where web indicates that this process is a web process, gunicorn is the WSGI server you're using, app is the name of your Flask application file, and the second app is the name of the Flask application instance within that file. This tells Heroku how to start your application when it receives incoming web requests. Without a Procfile, the deployment platform wouldn't know how to launch your application.

The requirements.txt file lists all the Python packages that your application depends on. When you deploy your application, the deployment platform uses this file to install all the necessary dependencies, ensuring that your application has access to all the libraries it needs to run correctly. Imagine your application using Flask-WTF for forms, SQLAlchemy for database interaction, and requests for making HTTP requests. All these packages need to be installed in the deployment environment. You create the requirements.txt file by running pip freeze > requirements.txt in your local development environment. This command captures all the packages and their versions that are currently installed in your virtual environment and saves them to the requirements.txt file. When you deploy your application, the platform will typically run pip install -r requirements.txt to install all the required packages.

A common question is, "Why not just install the packages manually on the server?" While technically possible, this is highly impractical and error-prone. The requirements.txt file provides a standardized and reproducible way to manage dependencies. It ensures that all the required packages, and the correct versions, are installed on the server, preventing dependency conflicts and ensuring consistency between development and production environments. Another question is, "What if my application doesn't have any external dependencies?" Even if your application doesn't directly use any external packages, it's still a good practice to create an empty requirements.txt file. This signals to the deployment platform that you have considered dependencies, even if there are none at the moment. Preparing these files before deployment is essential for a smooth and successful deployment process. They provide the necessary instructions and dependency information for the deployment platform to run your application correctly.

DEPLOYING TO HEROKU

Deploying a Flask application to Heroku involves several steps, transforming your local development project into a live, accessible web application. First, ensure you have a Heroku account and the Heroku CLI (Command Line Interface) installed on your machine. Initialize a Git repository in your project directory if you haven't already, as Heroku uses Git for deployments. Next, create a Procfile in your project's root directory. This file tells Heroku how to run your application. For a typical Flask app using Gunicorn, the Procfile would contain the line web: gunicorn app:app, assuming your main Flask file is named app.py and your Flask application instance is also named app. If your application uses a different WSGI server or has a different file/instance naming convention, adjust the Procfile accordingly.

A requirements.txt file is essential. Create it by running pip freeze > requirements.txt in your virtual environment. This file lists all your project's Python dependencies, ensuring Heroku installs the correct packages. Create a Heroku app through the Heroku website or CLI (heroku create). This allocates a space for your application on Heroku's servers. Then, add Heroku as a Git remote: heroku git:remote -a your-app-name, replacing your-app-name with the name of your Heroku app.

Now, the deployment process is as simple as pushing your code to the Heroku remote: git push heroku main (or git push heroku master depending on your Git branch). Heroku will automatically detect your Flask application, install the dependencies listed in requirements.txt, and start your application using the instructions in the Procfile.

After the push completes, you can open your application in your browser using heroku open. This should launch your Flask application running live on Heroku. A common question is, "What if my application uses environment variables?" Heroku provides a way to set environment variables through the Heroku dashboard or CLI (heroku config:set VARIABLE_NAME=value). These environment variables can then be accessed within your Flask application using os.environ. Another question is, "How do I manage database migrations on Heroku?" If your application uses a database, you'll need to migrate the database schema after deploying. Heroku provides various ways to do this, depending on the database you're using. For example, if you're using PostgreSQL, you might use heroku run python manage.py db upgrade (assuming you're using Flask-Migrate). Deploying to Heroku streamlines the process of making your Flask application accessible online. By following these steps and addressing

common issues, you can quickly and easily deploy your Flask projects.

DEPLOYING TO OTHER PLATFORMS

While Heroku is a popular choice for deploying Flask applications, other platforms offer compelling alternatives, each with its own strengths and weaknesses. PythonAnywhere, for instance, is a platform specifically designed for hosting Python applications, including Flask. It simplifies the deployment process significantly, particularly for beginners, by providing a user-friendly web interface and handling much of the server configuration behind the scenes. Imagine building a simple web application for personal use or a small project; PythonAnywhere's ease of use makes it an attractive option. Deploying to PythonAnywhere typically involves creating an account, setting up a web application project, and then uploading your Flask application code, along with any necessary dependencies. PythonAnywhere provides different ways to upload your code, such as using a web-based file manager or connecting via SSH.

One of the key advantages of PythonAnywhere is its simplicity. It handles the web server configuration, so you don't need to worry about setting up Gunicorn or other WSGI servers. You simply upload your code, configure a few settings, and your application is live. PythonAnywhere also provides a built-in editor and console, making it convenient to develop and debug your applications directly on the platform. However, PythonAnywhere might offer less flexibility and control compared to platforms like AWS or Google Cloud Platform. For larger, more complex applications with specific infrastructure requirements, a platform that gives you more direct access to the server environment might be more suitable. Another platform worth mentioning is Google App Engine, which is particularly well-suited for applications that integrate with other Google services. App Engine offers automatic scaling and a managed environment, simplifying deployment and maintenance. However, it might have a steeper learning curve compared to PythonAnywhere, and it might be more cost-effective for certain types of applications. Choosing the right deployment platform depends on your application's specific needs, your technical expertise, and your budget. PythonAnywhere is a great option for simpler projects where ease of use is a priority, while other platforms offer more control and flexibility for larger, more complex applications.

DOMAIN NAME SETUP

Setting up a custom domain name for your deployed application is the final touch that gives it a professional and recognizable online presence. Instead of users accessing your application through a platform-provided URL (like your-app-name.herokuapp.com or your-app.pythonanywhere.com), a custom domain (like www.your-website.com) makes your application more memorable and reinforces your brand. The process generally involves two key steps: first, configuring your domain registrar (like GoDaddy, Namecheap, or Google Domains) and second, configuring your hosting platform (like Heroku, PythonAnywhere, or AWS).

At your domain registrar, you'll typically create a CNAME record or an A record. A CNAME record points your custom domain (or a subdomain, like www) to the hostname provided by your hosting platform. For example, you might create a CNAME record that points www.your-website.com to your-app-name.herokuapp.com. An A record, on the other hand, points your domain to the IP address of your hosting server. Your hosting platform will provide you with either the hostname (for CNAME) or the IP address (for A record) that you need to use at your domain registrar. The specific steps for creating these records vary slightly depending on your domain registrar's interface, but the general principle is the same.

Once you've configured your domain registrar, you need to configure your hosting platform to recognize your custom domain. Most platforms provide settings within their control panel or dashboard where you can add your custom domain. You'll typically need to verify that you own the domain, often by adding a specific DNS record provided by the hosting platform. After verification, the hosting platform will configure its servers to respond to requests for your custom domain, directing traffic to your application. A common question is, "How long does it take for the custom domain to start working?" DNS propagation, the process of updating DNS records across the internet, can take anywhere from a few minutes to 48 hours (or, in rare cases, even longer). This means that it might take some time before your custom domain starts resolving to your application. Another question is, "Can I use both a custom domain and the platform-provided URL?" Yes, typically you can. Users will be able to access your application using either URL, but it's generally recommended to redirect the platform-provided URL to your custom domain to avoid duplicate content issues and improve SEO. Setting up a custom domain is a crucial step in branding your web application and making it more accessible to users. It provides a professional touch and enhances your online presence.

EXERCISE

Let's put our deployment knowledge into practice with a hands-on exercise: deploying our Flask application to a platform of our choice and configuring a custom domain name. Imagine we've built a polished Flask web application, perhaps a blog, a portfolio site, or a simple e-commerce application, and we're ready to share it with the world. This exercise will walk through the process of deploying the application to a platform like Heroku, PythonAnywhere, or a similar service and then connecting it to a custom domain name. First, we'll choose a deployment platform based on our project's needs and our comfort level. For smaller projects or for learning, Heroku or PythonAnywhere might be excellent starting points due to their ease of use. For larger or more complex projects, AWS or Google Cloud might be more appropriate, albeit with a steeper learning curve.

Next, we'll prepare our application for deployment. This includes creating a Procfile to instruct the platform on how to run our application, generating a requirements.txt file to list all the required Python packages, and ensuring our application code is clean and well-organized. We'll then follow the specific deployment steps for our chosen platform. For Heroku, this would involve initializing a Git repository, creating a Heroku app, and pushing our code to the Heroku remote. For PythonAnywhere, this would involve creating a web app project and uploading our code through their interface. For other platforms, the process will vary, but it generally involves uploading our code, configuring the server environment, and starting the application.

Once our application is deployed and running on the platform's provided URL, we'll set up a custom domain name. This involves two parts. First, we'll go to our domain registrar (like GoDaddy, Namecheap, or Google Domains) and create a CNAME record (or an A record, depending on the platform's instructions) that points our custom domain (e.g., www.my-awesome-app.com) to the URL provided by the deployment platform. Second, we'll go to our deployment platform's control panel and add our custom domain to the application settings. This step usually involves verifying that we own the domain by adding a specific DNS record. After both steps are completed, and after DNS propagation (which can take a few minutes to a few hours), our application should be accessible through our custom domain name. This exercise provides a valuable, real-world experience in deploying a Flask application and configuring a custom domain, the final steps in making our web application live and accessible to the public.

CHAPTER 12

BEST PRACTICES

CODE ORGANIZATION AND STRUCTURE

Structuring a Flask project effectively is crucial for long-term maintainability and scalability, especially as the application grows in complexity. A well-organized project makes it easier for developers to understand the codebase, add new features, and debug issues. A flat, unstructured project, on the other hand, can quickly become a tangled mess, making it difficult to navigate and maintain. A recommended approach is to organize your Flask project into logical modules or packages. This involves separating different parts of your application, such as models, forms, views, and utilities, into separate files and directories. For example, you might have a models directory containing your database models, a forms directory for your Flask-WTF forms, and a views directory for your view functions. This modular structure makes it clear where to find specific parts of the code and promotes code reusability.

Blueprints in Flask provide a way to further organize your application into reusable components. A blueprint is essentially a mini-application that can be registered with the main Flask application. This allows you to create modular and independent parts of your application, each with its own routes, templates, and static files. Imagine building a large e-commerce website; you might have separate blueprints for product management, user accounts, shopping cart, and checkout. Each blueprint can be developed and tested independently, and they can be easily plugged into the main application. Blueprints also help with namespace management, preventing naming conflicts between different parts of the application. Furthermore, they can improve code organization by grouping related functionality together.

A common question is, "When should I use blueprints?" Blueprints are particularly useful for larger applications with multiple developers or when you have distinct sections within your application that could potentially be reused in other projects. For smaller projects, you might not need blueprints initially, but it's a good practice to structure your code in a modular way so that you can easily introduce blueprints later if needed. Another question is, "How do I register blueprints with my Flask application?" You register blueprints using the app.register_blueprint() method. You can also specify a URL prefix for each blueprint, allowing you to mount them at different URLs. For example, you might register a blueprint for user accounts at the

/accounts prefix. Structuring your Flask projects effectively using modularization and blueprints is essential for building maintainable and scalable web applications. It improves code organization, promotes reusability, and simplifies development and collaboration.

SECURITY BEST PRACTICES

Web application security is paramount, and Flask applications are no exception. Several common vulnerabilities can expose your application to attacks, compromising user data and potentially bringing down your entire system. Cross-Site Scripting (XSS) is a vulnerability that allows attackers to inject malicious JavaScript code into web pages viewed by other users. Imagine a forum where users can post comments. If the forum doesn't properly sanitize user input, an attacker could inject JavaScript code into a comment that, when viewed by other users, executes in their browsers. This code could steal cookies, redirect users to malicious websites, or even deface the forum. Preventing XSS involves carefully sanitizing all user input before displaying it on the page. Flask's templating engine automatically escapes HTML by default, which helps, but you need to be particularly careful when displaying user-provided data directly, especially if you're using JavaScript to dynamically update content.

SQL injection is another critical vulnerability that occurs when user-provided input is directly embedded into SQL queries. An attacker can craft malicious input that modifies the SQL query, potentially gaining access to the entire database or even executing arbitrary commands on the server. Imagine a website that allows users to search for products. If the search term is directly inserted into the SQL query, an attacker could enter a malicious search term that alters the query to return all products instead of just the ones matching the search. Preventing SQL injection requires using parameterized queries or prepared statements. These techniques treat user input as data, not as executable code, effectively preventing attackers from manipulating the query. Flask libraries like Flask-SQLAlchemy handle this for you automatically, provided you use their query methods correctly.

Cross-Site Request Forgery (CSRF) is an attack where a malicious website tricks a user's browser into making an unwanted request to another website where the user is currently authenticated. Imagine a user logged in to their bank's website. A malicious website could contain a hidden form that automatically submits a request to the bank's website to transfer money from the user's account. If the bank's website doesn't have proper CSRF protection, this request could succeed. CSRF protection typically involves including a unique, unpredictable token in each form submitted by the user. This token is then verified by the server to ensure that the request originated from the legitimate form. Flask-WTF provides built-in CSRF protection, making it easy to implement this crucial security measure in your Flask applications. Addressing these common vulnerabilities through proper input sanitization, parameterized queries, and CSRF protection is essential for building secure and reliable web applications. Regularly reviewing security best practices and staying up-to-date on the latest vulnerabilities is crucial for maintaining a secure application.

PERFORMANCE OPTIMIZATION

Optimizing the performance of Flask applications is crucial for providing a smooth and responsive user experience, especially as the application scales. Several techniques can be employed to improve performance, focusing on different aspects of the application. Caching is a powerful technique that stores frequently accessed data in memory, reducing the need to repeatedly fetch it from slower sources like databases or external APIs. Imagine a popular blog post; instead of querying the database every time a user views the post, you can cache the rendered HTML output. Subsequent requests can be served directly from the cache, significantly reducing server load and improving response times. Flask provides several ways to implement caching, from simple in-memory caching using Flask's cache object to more sophisticated caching solutions using Redis or Memcached. Choosing the right caching strategy depends on the application's needs and traffic patterns.

Database optimization is another critical area for performance improvement. Slow database queries can significantly impact application performance. Techniques like indexing, query optimization, and connection pooling can dramatically improve database performance. Imagine an e-commerce platform with a large product catalog; proper indexing of the product table can significantly speed up product searches. Connection pooling reuses database connections, reducing the overhead of establishing new connections for every request. Profiling your database queries can help identify slow queries that need optimization. Furthermore, the way you structure your database models and relationships can impact performance. Choosing the right database and using appropriate data types can also contribute to better performance.

Beyond caching and database optimization, several other performance considerations are important. Minifying and compressing static assets (CSS, JavaScript, images) reduces the amount of data that needs to be transferred over the network, improving page load times. Using a Content Delivery Network (CDN) to serve static assets can further reduce latency, especially for users geographically distant from your server. Asynchronous tasks, implemented using Celery or Redis Queue, allow you to offload long-running tasks from the main request thread, preventing your application from becoming unresponsive. For example, sending emails or processing large datasets can be handled asynchronously. Profiling your application's code can help identify performance bottlenecks. Tools like cProfile can analyze your code's execution and pinpoint areas where it's spending excessive time. Finally, choosing the right WSGI server (like Gunicorn or uWSGI) and properly configuring your web server (like Nginx or Apache) are crucial for handling concurrent requests efficiently. Optimizing Flask applications is an ongoing process, and a holistic approach that considers all aspects of the application is key to achieving optimal performance.

FLASK EXTENSIONS

Flask's extensibility is one of its greatest strengths, allowing developers to easily integrate powerful features and functionalities into their applications. Flask extensions provide pre-built solutions for common tasks, saving development time and effort. Several extensions have become particularly popular due to their widespread use and the value they bring to Flask development. Flask-SQLAlchemy, for instance, is an Object-Relational Mapper (ORM) that simplifies database interactions. Imagine building a web application that needs to store and retrieve data from a database. Instead of writing raw SQL queries, Flask-SQLAlchemy allows you to define your database tables as Python classes (models) and then interact with the database using object-oriented methods. This abstraction makes database interactions more intuitive and less prone to SQL injection vulnerabilities. Flask-SQLAlchemy supports various database systems, allowing you to easily switch between them if needed.

Flask-WTF simplifies web form handling. Building and validating forms can be a tedious process, especially for complex forms with multiple fields and validation rules. Flask-WTF provides a structured way to define forms as Python classes, making form creation, rendering, and validation much easier. It also provides built-in CSRF protection, a crucial security measure. Think of building a user registration form; Flask-WTF streamlines the process of defining the form fields, validating user input (e.g., checking for valid email addresses or password strength), and handling form submissions. Flask-Login manages user authentication. Implementing user login, logout, and session management can be complex and requires careful attention to security. Flask-Login provides a robust and well-tested solution for handling these tasks, freeing developers from reinventing the wheel and reducing the risk of introducing security vulnerabilities. Imagine building a web application that requires users to log in; Flask-Login provides the tools to manage user sessions, protect routes, and implement "remember me" functionality.

A common question is, "Why should I use Flask extensions instead of writing my own code for these functionalities?" Flask extensions are typically well-maintained, thoroughly tested, and widely used, which means they are less likely to contain bugs and have been vetted by the community. They also provide a consistent and standardized way to implement common functionalities, making it easier for developers to collaborate and understand each other's code. Another question is, "How do I install and use Flask extensions?" You can install Flask extensions using pip, just like any other Python package. Once installed, you typically import the extension into your Flask application and initialize it. The specific usage instructions vary depending on the extension, but the documentation for each extension provides clear guidance. Using Flask extensions is a best practice for building robust and efficient Flask applications. They save development time, improve code quality, and enhance security.

REFERENCES

[1] Bernstein, D. J. (2000). Strengthening password hashes. CryptoBytes, 3(3), 1-3.

[2] Chacon, S., & Straub, B. (2014). Pro Git. Apress.

[3] Chodorow, K. (2010). MongoDB: The definitive guide. O'Reilly Media, Inc.

[4] Fielding, R. T. (2000). Architectural styles and the design of network-based software architectures. (Doctoral dissertation, University of California, Irvine).

[5] Fielding, R., Gettys, J., Mogul, J., Frystyk, H., Masinter, L., Leach, P., & Berners-Lee, T. (1999). Hypertext Transfer Protocol -- HTTP/1.1. RFC 2616.1

[6] High Scalability. (2011, November 21). Pinterest Architecture: 100s of Millions of Users, Terabytes of Data and Hundreds of Engineers. Retrieved from High Scalability

[7] Lattner, C. (2015). Django: Web Development Made Easy. Apress.

[8] OWASP. (2023). Cross-Site Scripting (XSS). Retrieved from OWASP

[9] Provos, N., & Mazieres, D. (2007). A low-cost defense against dictionary and brute-force attacks. USENIX.

[10] Python Packaging Authority. (n.d.). venv - Creating Virtual Environments. Retrieved from Python Documentation

[11] Richardson, L., & Ruby, S. (2002). RESTful web services. Addison-Wesley Professional.

[12] Sadalage, P. J., & Fowler, M. (2012). NoSQL distilled: A brief guide to the emerging world of polyglot persistence. Addison-Wesley Professional.

[13] Silberschatz, A., Korth, H. F., & Sudarshan, S. (2010). Database system concepts. McGraw-Hill.

[14] Stonebraker, M., & Neuhold, E. J. (2010). Distributed database systems. Springer Science & Business Media.

[15] The Pallets Projects. (n.d.). Deploying Flask. Retrieved from Flask Documentation

This page is intentionally left blank.

ABOUT THE AUTHOR

Mark John Lado is an accomplished Information System Specialist with a strong background in education and technology. He holds a Master's degree in Information Technology from Northern Negros State College of Science and Technology and is currently pursuing his Doctorate in the same field.

Mark boasts a diverse professional experience, having served as an ICT Instructor/Coordinator at Carmen Christian School Inc., a Part-time Information Technology Instructor at the University of the Visayas, and a Faculty member at Colegio de San Antonio de Padua and Cebu Technological University. He is currently a Faculty member at the College of Technology and Engineering at Cebu Technological University.

His expertise extends beyond the classroom, encompassing Object-Oriented Programming, Teacher Mentoring, Computer Hardware, Software System Analysis, and Web Development. He actively participates in the Philippine Society of Information Technology Educators (PSITE) as a member and has contributed to the academic community through the publication of his research article, "A Wireless Digital Public Address with Voice Alarm and Text-to-speech Feature for Different Campuses," in Globus An International Journal of Management & IT.

Mark's dedication to education and passion for technology are evident in his contributions to various educational institutions, including Cebu Technological University, University of the Visayas - Danao Campus, Colegio de San Antonio de Padua, and Carmen Christian School Inc.

Biography Source:

Mark John Lado. (n.d.). *Biographies.net.* Retrieved January 24, 2025, from https://www.biographies.net/

Authors' Official Website:

https://markjohnlado.com/

This page is intentionally left blank.

www.ingramcontent.com/pod-product-compliance
Lightning Source LLC
Chambersburg PA
CBHW070945050326
40689CB00014B/3346